LESSONS FROM THE STORIES OF THE QUR'AN

By
ALI MUSA RAZA MUHAJIR

Foreword by
Dr. M. Hamidullah

kiTAB BHAVAN
New Delhi-110002

Kitab Bhavan
Publishers, Distributors, Exporters & Importers
1784, Kalan Mahal, Darya Ganj
New Delhi - 1100 02 (India)

Phone   : (91-11) 23277392/93, 23274686, 30906494
website : www.kitabbhavan.com
Email   : nasri@vsnl.com
Fax   : (91-11) 23263383

First Edition   1965
Second Revised Edition   1992
Third Reprinted   2005

ISBN   : 81-7151-166-X
Code No. : L00036

Laser Typesetting at :
Laser Track,
Kalan Mahal, Darya Ganj
New Delhi - 1100 02

Published in India by :
Nusrat Ali Nasri for Kitab Bhavan
1784, Kalan Mahal, Darya Ganj
New Delhi - 1100 02 [India]

Printed in India at :
Nice Printing Press
Khureji Khas, Delhi-110051

CONTENTS

FOREWORD

It is an honour to me to be asked to write a foreword to the work of an erudite author, from whom during my student days I have learnt many things by which I am still profiting.

The Judeo-Christian authors have so much produced on Islam and on the venerated Prophet of Islam that it is time that Muslims too think of beginning to repay the debt. The Judeo-Christians will certainly profit by a perusal of this book which, far from being a polemic against them, is an attempt to reglorify the names so dear to them. For every Muslim believes in the Prophets of yore as he believes in Muhammad (sallal-lahu'alaihi-wa-sallam).

Truth and nothing but truth is the ultimate goal of every searcher in matters religious. Stress can never be laid too much on the fact that one must interest in the question: wherefrom do I come?--in order to distinguish oneself from mere animals and beasts who, like us, eat, drink, sleep, multiply themselves and die. Religious question is no more a *la mode*, but need is there that someone tells us that we are neglecting our duties to our own selves.

It is rare to find among Muslims such authors as simultaneously are well versed in both Qur'anic and Biblical lores. In dealing with the stories of the Biblical and other Prophets the author has shown a comprehensive grasp of the subject and has tried to remove the misconceptions the Bible creates about these holy personages in the mind of its readers. I am sure, the reader will greatly profit by the vast amount of knowledge collected in this book.

M. Hamidullah

Paris
18 Jamadi-ul-Awwal, 1381

INTRODUCTION

God as declared by Himself in the Qur'an is the *Rabbul-'Alamin*, the Creator, Evolver, Sustainer and Cherisher of all the creatures and everything else in the world. His providence encompasses not only the entire physical side of human beings but it also furnishes them with the means of spiritual sustenance to enable them to attain to the ideal of becoming his vicegerents on earth. For this reason Prophets were raised who, by their teachings, preachings, and their practical application to life, tried to guide mankind in the proper use of everything made available to it by God for realising that ideal. Man by the use of his intellect, as mentioned in connection with Adam in the Qur'an, cannot reach this stage of perfection by himself. Therefore it was said:

(1) When there comes to you a guidance from Me, then whoso follows My guidance, no fear shall be on them, nor shall they grieve. And those who choose disbelief and belie Our signs, these be the companions of fire; in that they abide (ii. 38-39).

As these Prophets were raised to guide men to attain their perfection, it was necessary that they themselves should be perfect specimens of humanity to serve as models to and reformers of mankind. The Qur'an says that:

(*i*) All nations of the world were provided with spiritual guidance through their Prophets:

(2) And every community had its warner (xxxv. 24).

(3) And for each community there was a messenger (x. 47).

(*ii*) These Prophets were all human beings, as human beings only could serve as perfect models to and reformers of mankind:

(4) And nothing prevents men from believing when the guidance comes to them except that they say: Does God raise up a human being as a messenger? Say: Had there been in the earth angels walking therein as settlers, surely We would have caused to come down upon them from above an angel as a messenger (xvii. 94-95).

(5) And We sent not before thee except men whom We gave

Our command. Therefore ask ye of the people of the Book if you know not. And We gave them not bodies not taking food and they were not exempt from death (xxi. 7-8).

(*iii*) All these Prophets were sinless:

(6) It is not attributable to a prophet that he should act unfaithfully (iii. 160).

(*iv*) They were all given books for the guidance of their people:

(7) Then God sends His Prophets (*Anbiya*), bearers of glad tidings and so warners, and He sends with them the Book with the truth (ii. 213).

(8) Surely We have sent Our messengers (*Rusul*) with clear proofs and We have sent down with them the Book and the balance that mankind may keep up justice (lvii. 25).

(*v*) Only some among them were mentioned by name but there were many more whose names were not mentioned:

(9) And there are messengers We have related to thee ere this and messengers We have not related to thee (iv. 164).

(*vi*) Belief in the Prophets of all nations is an essential article of a Muslim's faith and forms the basis of the brotherhood of all nations:

(10) And who believe in what has been sent to thee and what was sent before thee (ii. 4).

In our book entitled *Tenets of Islam* under the heading "Belief in Prophets" we have dealt fully with this subject. We refer the reader to it for further elucidation.

The Qur'an is not a book of history or biography. When referring to the Prophets the Qur'an speaks of their work for the grand object of reformation, their particular traits, the reactions of their people to their teachings and of the extent of their success to establish truth and uprooting evil. Mostly such incidents are chosen from their lives as contained parallel to what happened in the life of Muhammad (may his religion prevail) and which could bring comfort and solace to the Prophet and his followers in facing persecution and its consequent distress, confirming from the illustrations of previous sacred history that truth shall ultimately be established and opposition fail.

(11) These are announcements relating to the unseen which We reveal to thee. Thou didst not know them, neither thou nor thy people before this. Therefore be patient: surely the end is for those who are righteous (xi. 40).

(12) And all We related to thee of the accounts of the apostles is to strengthen thy heart therewith and in this has come to thee the truth and admonition and a reminder to the believers (xi. 120).

(13) And those who disbelieve say: Why has not the Qur'an been revealed to him all at once. Just so, in order that We may steady thy heart therewith, and We have arranged it well in arranging (xxv. 32).

The Qur'an does not concern itself with the details of the lives of these Prophets. It only lays stress on one fact that all Prophets delivered the message of Unity of the Divine Being and invited their people to obey this Being and do good to fellow-men.

In narrating these stories the Qur'an has brought out facts which enhance the moral value of these narratives and remove the defects and contradictions which have found way into sacred history due to manipulation of facts or carelessness in recording them. Whatever slur is cast on the character of a Prophet in the narratives of the Bible or Jewish and Christian tradition, the Qur'an has invariably vindicated it. This affords the clearest evidence that Divine inspiration and not any previous record or tradition was the source from which the Holy Prophet obtained information. By doing away with the profanity of sacred history, the Qur'an has done immeasurable service to the Bible itself. This fact is hinted at in the following verses of the Qur'an:

(14) In their histories there is certainly a lesson for men of understanding. It is not a narrative which could be forget but a verification of what is before it and distinct explanation of all things and a guide and a mercy to a people who believe (xii. 111).

(15) We relate to thee their story with truth (xviii. 13).

(16) We relate to thee the best of stories by revealing to thee this Qur'an though before this thou wast certainly of the unaware ones (xii. 3).

(17) Thus do We recite to thee the histories of what passed of old and indeed We have given to thee a Reminder from Ourselves (xx. 99).

The above-quoted verses of the Qur'an must indeed be enough to satisfy that modernised section of the Muslims who are the advocates of "Liberal Islam" being awed by the Western civilisation and thought, and having not studied the Qur'an properly, that the Prophet did not make use of traditions of his time in the narratives he gave of the Prophets, but that the incidents referred to by him were, before his inspiration came, unknown to the Prophet and his audiences alike, and that what he said about these Prophets was the absolute truth delivered to him through the medium of God's angel Gabriel.

There are also people who feel that by the repetition of same incidents in these stories of the Prophets a sort of redundance, a disqualification in their estimation, has been created in the true word of God. It is wholly a misconception. Repetition in the Qur'an has a purpose of its own. The Qur'an was not written as a book by somebody sitting in a cloister. It is the record of collected open-air sermons by a man who was inspired by the Holy Spirit. His audience on every occasion consisted of different people, each of whom was entitled to learn what was told to the others before. Such things as had to be emphasised and driven deep into the hearts of the listeners had to be repeated. The Qur'an is the best example of highly effective rhetoric. So the repetition; but they are so dovetailed within other items that if we place them all in one place they will not be a tautological discourse. Something new is found in every repetition if examined with reference to its context.

The modern Christian and other critics of the Qur'an audaciously assert that the sources of the information of the Prophet were the Bible or those Jews and Christians of his time who came into contact with him. Let us now examine if there is any truth at all in these allegations.

The Qur'anic concept of God in its sublime purity and majesty is so radically different from the ridiculous and horribly unclean conception given by the Bible that one having no bias is constrained to admit that Muhammad could possibly have no inspiration from the Bible or the Jews or the Christians of his time. He would have thrown the Bible away if he could have ever read a chapter of Exodus, Deuternomy or the gospels. But he had no access to the Bible. It was not translated in his time into Arabic. He could not have reproduced the Bible stories on the basis of hearsay, for the stories given by him are partly confirmed by the Bible and partly by those writings which the Jews and Christians of that time preserved as non-canonial and apocryphal secrets, and at the same time avoided their manipulations and blasphemies. As a matter of fact he came into contact with the Jews in his later days in Madinah where their relations were never cordial but on a war-footing, and he had given mostly the facts about the former Prophets before that time.

No religion can be based on documents which portray its own Prophets, leaders and religious men is Satanic colours. For example, the Bible speaks of deceit and lies attributed to Abraham, cheating and treachery to Issac and Jacob, adultery to David, incest to Lot, idol-worship to Aaron, apostasy to Solomon, and inhuman brutalities to Moses and Joshua, and at the same time calls all of them men after God's own heart, pointing unconsciously perhaps to the defect in God Himself of approving nefarious and heinous practices.

In the course of the accounts given of the Prophets in this book as narrated by the Qur'an, we have shown in detail all those calumnies which the Bible heaps up on the holy character of the Prophets and of which the Qur'an clears them. This is a further proof that the Qur'an does not borrow its material from the Bible or the Jewish literature.

In clear contract to these contaminated Biblical accounts stand the pure sublime theism and the practical code of morals contained in the Qur'an, proving that it could not have been derived from either the Jews or the Christians. *The Jews of his time never claimed to be Muhammad's teachers nor did the Christians of his day,* and no twisting of historical facts has been successful in proving this claim. The great historian Gibbon had to admit that no such thing could have ever happened. He says:

The Christians of the seventh century had insensibly relapsed into a semblance of paganism; their private and public vows were addressed to the relics and images that disgraced the temples of the East. The throne of the Almighty was darkened by a crowd of martyrs, saints and angels, the objects of popular veneration, and the Collyridian heretics who flourished in the fruitful soil of Arabia invested the virgin Mary with the name and honours of a goddess. The mysteries of the Trinity and Incarnation appeared to contradict the principle of the Divine Unity. In their obvious sense they introduced three equal deities and transformed the man Jesus into the substance of the Son of God. ...The creed of

Muhammad is free from the suspicion of ambiguity and the Qur'an is a glorious testimony to the Unity of God.

He goes on further to say:

Could such people ever approach the conception of the God of Muhammad which, as may be gathered from the several passages of the Qur'an is to this day so far above the ideal of Christianity and other religions in spite of reforms and revivals? There is no book in the world in which God has been made such a theme of discourse as in the holy Qur'an.

It is impossible to conceive aught holier, nobler, purer, more sublime, more perfect, more supreme and more worthy of the Godhead than the God whom Muhammad worshipped. The ideal cannot be improved upon: one attribute taken from it would marits perfection, and not one could be added to it that would not be superfluous. Such is the lofty conception of Muhammad's God as presented in the Qur'an. He has boldly and indelibly impressed the notion of the strictest monotheism upon the pages of history and towards this notion rational man cannot but drift surely if slowly.

There are other aspects to be considered besides the conception of God which prove conclusively that the Qur'an was nothing less than the true word of the All-Knowing God of the universe.

Scientific verities and discoveries or even theories of the modern scientific age were quite unknown in the days of the Prophet. But the Qur'an abounds with passages which contain scientific facts in the realms of astronomy, geology, biology, geography, zoology, archaeology and ancient history and incidentally there are prophecies of coming events predicted, which have been fulfilled or are being fulfilled. To enumerate these facts the space of an introduction cannot be sufficient. This on fact itself is enough to prove that the Prophet was Divinely inspired and what he spoke cannot be fibs and foibles of his own imagination. To give a glimpse of these scientific verities we quote below a few passage from the Qur'an:

(18) We have sent down the iron wherein there is great violence and advantages to men (lvii. 25).

Before the discovery of iron, this precious metal actually dropped from the heavens only in the form of materiorites, Man learnt slowly how to make use of iron for offensive purposes but

the modern age of iron and steel, which has made life so happy
and convenient, was never dreamt of in the age when this verse
was revealed.

(19) Consider the broadcaster when he broadcasts, and the
raisers of the heavy loads when they raise it up, and the
gliders gliding swiftly (on earth) and those who apportion
mandates... and the heavens full or orbits (lvii. 1-7).

A clear picture indeed of the modern age of invention and
technology which should never have occurred to any even a dream
in the days of the Prophet.

(20) And the sun moves on in its appointed axis that is the
ordinance of the Mighty, the Knowing, and for the moon,
We have ordained stages till it becomes again as an old
day palm branch....and all float in their respective orbits
(xxxvi. 38-40).

Facts relating to modern astronomy discovered through modern
telescopes which an astronomer only can fully appreciate and yet
announced by a Prophet who never knew even how to read or
write.

(21) ....and We have created for them the like of what you ride
upon (xxxvi. 42).

A prophetic allusion to the conveyances of travel that were
going to be used in later ages like the steam engine, the motor
car and the aeroplane.

(22) Lord of the two Easts and the two Wests (lv. 17).

This verse clearly indicates that the earth is a globe, a fact not
known to the world before the advent of Islam.

(23) God has created every living being from water (xxiv. 40).
A theory of modern biology and the evolution of life on earth.

(24) Glory be to Him Who created pairs of all things of what
the earth grows and of their own kind, and of what they
do not know (xxxvi. 36).

A modern discovery of the nature of things in the mineral,
vegetable and animal kingdoms.

In spite of these glaring facts the Christian critics have the
audacity to assert as gospel truth that the Prophet's inspiration was
based on the Bible accounts. Even a critic of the status of Sir William
Muir does not hesitate to mislead his readers when writing about
Islam and its founder. He writes:

Whether this "Witness" and the other Jewish supporters of Muhammad were among his professed followers, slaves *perhaps* at Mecca...*we can but conjecture*, whoever his Jewish friends *may have been*, it is evident that he had a knowledge of the outlines of Jewish history and tradition. These distorted by Rabbinical fables and embellished of travesties by the Prophet's fancy, supplied the material for the scriptural stories which at this period form a chief portion of the Qur'an (*Life of Muhammad*, p. 99). Mark the words italicised and the inferences derived.

There are other Christian critics of Islam who rely upon the following verses of the Qur'an as evidence of the fact that the Prophet borrowed his teachings from some followers of other faiths:

(25) And those who choose disbelief say: This is nothing but a lie which he has forged and other people have helped him therein. Then surely they have brought forth an injustice and a lie. And they say: Stories of the ancients which he has caused to be written so that they are read out to him morning and evening (xxv. 4-5).

(26) And most surely We know that they say: None but a man teaches him. The mother tongue of the man whom they refer to is foreign and this Qur'an is in clear Arabic tongue (xvi. 103).

The above verses are of Mecca origin and convey that the Meccan idolaters like modern Christian critics were puzzled as to what they could liken the Holy Qur'an. They knew him intimately and watched his movements closely and yet they could not advance their case beyond vague platitudes and mere conjectures. They, like the Christian critics of Islam, found it impossible to penetrate the mystery in which this subject was involved. Rodwell gives an explanation that it was in secrecy that the Prophet received his instructions. To admit in one place that "there were no secrets about his life" and to allege in the same breath that it was done in secrecy is to confess that there is no evidence in support of the allegation.

The mere mention of these allegations in the above-quoted verses has been taken as establishing their truth, but this proves nothing because the Qur'an refutes these allegations. If we analyse these verses we find that the Meccan idolaters did not know who the man was, but they knew he was not one of them, neither an

idolater nor an Arab. The denunciation of their idols by the Prophet
could not but lead them to this conclusion. The references to the
stories of the ancients indicate that they took this man to be a Jew
or a Christian of non-Arab origin, for they styled his tongue as
barbarous. The word used is *'Ajami* which signifies a non-Arab in
general and a Persian in particular. Again, these verses are of
Meccan origin and it is therefore reasonable to support that such
a man should have been associated with the Prophet both at Mecca
and Madinah, in other words, throughout his prophetic career. The
issue is thus narrowed down and we have to scrutinise in this light
and in keeping with the historical facts the various names
suggested by various non-Muslim writers on Islam:

(1) *Waraqah*, the aged cousin of Khadijah, cannot be the source
as suggested by some authors, as he died before the Prophet made
his mission public.

(2) *Mary the Capt*, the slave-girl sent by the rulers of Egypt
to the Prophet in response to his latter inviting him to Islam,
entered the household of the Prophet in 7H. Those who contend
that she tutored the Prophet in the Bible stories show their
ignorance of Islamic history.

(3) *Suhaib the Roman* was also alleged to be one of those from
whom it is probable that Muhammad gained some acquaintance
with Christianity. But they forget that after embracing Islam he
suffered much at the hands of the Quraish who did not allow him
to migrate until he relinquished all his wealth.

Is it conceivable that a man who willingly suffers and forgoes
his all to follow a homeless refugee (the Prophet) would blaspheme
the name of God and be a party to a fraud on humanity? The
character of Suhaib and his eventful life are in themselves
guarantees against his being guilty of any such charge.

(4) *Salman the Persian* is suggested by another Christian writer
and he bases his conjectures on the word *'Ajami*. But history records
that he met the Prophet at Quba' when the Prophet was migrating
to Madinah. Thus it is obvious that he was never with the Prophet
at Mecca before his flight and could not therefore have been the
person referred to in the Qur'an.

(5) *Qais or Kos the Bishop of Najran* whom the Prophet is said
to have met in his journey to Syria at the age of twelve is another
name suggested. But it is sheer nonsense to suggest that a boy

of this age could earn anything of religion and recollect and repeat at the age of forty what was narrated to him thirty years before.

(6) *Buhairah*, a Nestorian monk, is also suggested by some authors but Muir and Sale both reject this and Carlyle and Davenport consider this allegation as utterly baseless.

(7) *Some Christian slaves like Yasir, Jabar, etc.*, who were among the early converts to Islam are also suggested by some other authors. But the spirit which these slave converts displayed under severest torments is unique in history. The sincerity, the firmness and the resolution of these convert slaves, their readiness to suffer any loss, their willingness to undergo any hardship, are everlasting monuments of their living faith in the word of God and the Divine mission of the Prophet. It is preposterous to suggest that they had individually or collectively taught or even indicated to the Prophet what he should have put in the Book.

Another important argument refuting the allegation that Muhammad's knowledge came mainly from the hearsay of the Bible is the use of entirely different names of Biblical personages. Surely he could not have used different names for Biblical prophets if his knowledge had come direct from the Hebrews, unless they were known independently to the Arabs by such names. It cannot be suggested that the changes are due to adaptability of the Arabian accent in place of the Hebraic because both are sister languages with slight difference in the accent. Is it not then curious that the Prophet, in spite of learning everything from the Jews and the Christians, invents names of his own instead of their commonly known names of the Bible? We have given under footnotes explanations of some names used by the Qur'an in place of the Biblical names as far as possible within our reach.

Our readers by now must have seen how utterly baseless are the allegations that the so-called learned scholars of Christendom have made against that Prophet, simply because the Qur'an repeats some incidents of Jewish history with an entirely different purpose and mentions certain dogmas of Church Christianity, but they forget that while faithfully recording the story of any prophet and coherently too, it deviates from and omits that portion only which the Higher Biblical Criticism has found as the most unhistorical, absurd, and unworth in the story; for instance, the Qur'an does not endorse the Bible statements that God rested on the seventh

day of creation, the snake legend of the creation, temptation, the
union of the children of God with the daughters of man, Adam's
advent in historical times, and his genealogy, God walking in the
cool breeze of the evening, Cain protected from any harm being
done to him by men when he was the only man on earth, Noah's
worldwide flood and his wonderful menagerie of the Ark, Hagar
carrying the babe "sixteen years old" on her shoulders to settle
in the desert, the sun stopping in its ordit, etc. All these and many
more of a similar type along with the abominable picture of the
character of the Hebrew prophets, as already hinted above, would
have also decorated the pages of the Qur'an as they do those of
the Old Testament if the Bible had been the source of Muhammad's
inspiration.

The beauty of all is that what the Qur'an describes has been
corroborated by later research scholars thereby confirming the
claims of the Qur'an that its source is no other than Divine
revelation. This fact will be clearly noticed in the course of the
narratives of the Prophets that are the subject-matter of this book.

Among the stories of the Prophets we have omitted in this book
the stories of Jesus and Muhammad as given in the Qur'an for
they required a separate treatment, the former being a controversial
subject demanding elaborate explanation and the latter being the
central figurer round which all the material given in the Qur'an
revolves. They are, therefore, presented to the reading public in
two separate volumes under the title *Jesus in the Qur'an and
Muhammad as Depicted in the Qur'an*.

It is a well-known saying of the Arab scholars that the language
of the Qur'an is untranslatable. Yet for the benefit of those who
do not know Arabic, many scholars have attempted to give the
meaning of the Arabic text in their own language as closely as those
languages could afford to do. There are many English translations
of the Qur'an done by Muslim and non-Muslim scholars. The
version I have adopted in the translation of the Arabic text in this
book is mostly based on the following translations:

(1) 'Allamah 'Abdullah Yusuf 'Ali.

(2) M. Pickthall.

(3) Maulana Muhammad 'Ali.

As my version covers only the narrative portion of the Qur'anic
stories in which no basic beliefs of Islam are involved, I have taken

the liberty to interpret some of the verses in my own way to suit the context without prejudice to the original meaning of the text of the Qur'an.

Besides the verses of the Qur'an, much of the material used in this book by way of explanations is drawn from the writings of learned authors like Maulana Muhammad 'Ali and 'Allamah Yusuf 'Ali and I feel it my duty to put on record with thanks my indebtedness to these authors.

In the end I express my sincere thanks to Dr. M. Hamidullah, to prominent Muslim scholar and head of the Islamic Studies section of Paris University, for the Foreword he has given to this book.

Ali Musa Raza Muhajir

I

THE STORY OF ADAM

The story of the creation of man is told in the Qur'an in plain, simple words admissible to reason. His origin, his development, his nature, his progress in the world, his constant struggle with the forces of Evil and his ultimate destiny--all these verities are dispersed in the Qur'an and cover considerable portion of it. We have in this chapter attempted to collect them so as to give a coherent account of the whole episode.

1. The Creation of Adam

Adam, in other words man, was created from dust as is evident from the following verses:

(1) When your Lord said to the angels: Surely, I am going to create a mortal (Bashar) from dust (xxxviii. 71).

(2) O mankind! Surely We created you from dust (xxii. 5).

(3) He began the creation of man (Insan) from dust (xxii. 7).

(4) He created him [Adam] from dust (iii. 58).

(5) Dost thou disbelieve in Him Who created thee from dust (xviii. 37).

(6) And one of His signs is that He created you from dust (xxx. 20).

In all these verses the words Adam, Man (Insan), and Mortal (Bashar) are synonymous. Here Adam as well as all men (You) are spoken of as having been created from dust which is another term for primeval matter created from nothing by God, the Cause of all causes.

The word "Adam" is used in the Qur'an for man for the reason that he is a conglomeration of all the elements of the earth with all their inherent properties: "An extract of clay" as the Qur'an calls him (xxiii. 12). It is derived from the Arabic rootword Udmat which means "to mix".

Then it is said that man or Adam is created of dry clay, of black smelling mud, and of an extract of clay and is given a shape.

(7) And certainly We have made man out of dry clay, of black miry mud (xv. 26).

(8) And most surely We have made man from an extract of clay (xxiii. 12).

(9) Indeed We created you and fashioned you in due proportion (vii. II).

It is not correct to understand that the extract of clay is the same as black miry mud. The idea conveyed by the above two verses is not the same. The extract of clay must include all the elements that are found in the earth and, according to the latest researches, they are said to be one hundred and five in number and by a chemical analysis of the human body it is discovered that every one of those elements is found in an appropriate quantity, though some are in so small a quantity that their presence is not easily detected. When the quantity of any of these elements gets diminished, a disturbance is caused in the normal functioning of the body, and to restore normal health the doctor supplements this deficiency by giving an appropriate dose of what he calls vitamins.

If we understand that God made a statue of man of the potter's clay and by breathing into it. His spirit turned it into a living man, then it will be incorrect to say that he was made of an extract of clay. There is no mention anywhere in the Qur'an that man was brought into existence in this way all at once. On the other hand, there are verses in the Qur'an to denote that all life started from water, man being no exception.

(10) And We have made of water everything living (xxi. 50).

(11) And Allah has created from water every living creature, of them is that which moves upon its belly, and of them is that which walks upon four feet, and of them is that which walks upon two feet. Allah creates whom He pleases; surely God has power over all things (xxiv. 45).

(12) And He it is Who has created man from water (xxv. 54).

In quotation No. 7 it is said that God created man from miry clay (like that of the potter's) and in quotation No. 12 it is said that God created man out of water and in quotations No. 10 and 11 it is told that all living things were created from water (including man who also comes under the category of living things which walk on two legs). All these verses corroborate the theory of evolution which says that all life began in miry clay on the coasts of oceans and lakes.

To support the theory of evolution the attributive name of God mentioned in the Qur'an in the beginning of the opening chapter, namely, *Rabb*, conveys the meaning of one who creates a thing and then develops it taking it from stage to stage in order that it might attain its full stature of perfection. The law of Evolution conveys almost exactly the same idea and therefore it can be easily seen that *Rububiyah* is another expression for the law of Evolution.

If we look at the creatures of the world we shall notice that every living thing in the earliest stage of its existence is in its embryonic condition from which it slowly and gradually develops to its perfection.

(13) Allah is the creator of everything and He is in charge of the welfare of everything (xxxix. 62).

God is described here as *Vakil* of everything after its creation which means that He does not create anything whether living or without life in its perfect condition all at once, but after creating a thing carries it through a series of stages until it reaches its final stage of perfection. This does not mean that He has no power to create a thing in its perfect form. He can bring a full-grown man from a state of non-existence to a state of perfect existence all at once, but He does not do so, for in that case His attribute of *Rububiyah* will not function. All the laws of nature that are at work in the life of the universe are no more than the manifestations of His attributes and to think that His absolute Power, which is also one of His attributes, will go against His other attributes would amount to denying perfection to His attributes. That is why the Qur'an says that the laws of God are immutable.

(14) And you will not find a change in Our course (xvii. 77).

(15) And you will not find a change in the course of Allah (xxxiii. 62).

(16) And you shall not find any alteration in the course of Allah (xxx. 43).

Under this law of evolution the Qur'an describes the creation of man in the following words:

(17) And certainly We created man of an extract of clay; then We placed him in a drop of sperm in a place of rest firmly

fixed; then We made the sperm into a clot of congealed blood; then of the clot We made a lump (foetus); then We make out of that lump bones and clothed the bones with flesh; then We developed out of it another creature. So, blessed be Allah the best to create (xxiii. 12-14).

In this verse God's creative work, so far as man is concerned, is briefly described. It states that inorganic matter becomes organic and living matter. The inorganic constituents of the earth having been absorbed into living matter by way of food the living matter reproduces itself by means of sperm a genital of the male sex. It is deposited in the ovum and fertilises it and rests for a time in security in the mother's womb. Then the next stage in the fertilised ovum is its conversion into a sort of clot of thickly congealed blood; the zygote cells grow by segmentation; then the mass gradually assumes shape in its growth as a foetus. From the lump develop bones and organs and a nervous system.

II. Breathing of Divine Spirit

The development of another creature in the closing words of the above quotation shows a further process that takes place which gives the offspring human consciousness, in other words called "the breathing of God's Spirit".

(18) So when I have made him complete and breathed into him of My spirit, fall down making obeisance to him (xv. 29).

(19) Behold! Your Lord said to the angels: Surely I am going to create a mortal from dust. When I have made him complete and breathed into him of My spirit, fall ye down in obeisance¯ to him (xxxviii. 71-72).

The Divine spirit is breathed into man after he has been made physically complete. It means he has been endowed with the faculty of God-like knowledge and the power to discriminate between good and evil and a will to choose, which, if rightly used elevates him to the exalted office of the vicegerent of God on earth, to whom all the forces of nature are made subservient.

Mark the words in quotations No. 18 and 19: "When I have made him complete." Here the word used is *Taswiyah* which in Arabic indicates that the creation of man took place in several stages progressing from one lower to one higher stage until he was fit to receive the breath of the Divine Spirit.

The Qur'an clearly states that the creation of man began from dust:

(20) He began the creation of man from dust. Then He made his progeny of an extract of water held in light estimation. Then He made him complete and breathed into him of His spirit and made for you ears and eyes and heart (xxxii. 7-9).

When his body, through the process of progeniture by gradual progress, reached perfection, God breathed His spirit into him which gave him the faculty of hearing, seeing and reasoning. This gradual process of man's physical development is referred to again in the following verses:

(21) Indeed He has created you under various conditions...and Allah has made you grow out of the earth in the manner of a plant (lxxi. 14-18).

(22) He evolved you from the earth and caused you to dwell therein (xiv. 61).

Here the word *Kum* in Arabic meaning "You" is used indicating the whole race of mankind, and it is pointed out that they had to pass through various conditions and they were evolved (*Nushu*) from the earth and made to grow in the manner of a tree. Thus God compares man's creation and evolution with the growth of a tree. The origin of a tree is a small seed having the potentially to grow into a huge tree but to reach to that stature it has to pass through numerous stages. Same is the case with everything on this earth; the only difference is that the evolutionary process of certain things takes place before our eyes and there are many things whose evolutionary process reached its perfection even before man was born on the earth. The solar system, the earth, its water, its animal life, etc., had their own evolutionary periods which can be deduced from the following verses of the Qur'an:

(23) Do not those who choose disbelief see that the heavens and the earth were bound up together but We have opened them and have made of water everything living (xxi. 30).

(24) And Allah's throne (i.e., His rule) was on water (xi. 7).

(25) Say: What! Do you indeed disbelieve in Him Who created the earth in two periods....and He made therein its food in four periods. This is (an explanation) equally (clear) to all who inquire. Then He directed Himself to the space above and it was a mere gas, so He said to it and to the

earth: Come both willingly or unwillingly. They both said: We come willingly. Then He finished them into seven heavenly bodies in two periods (xli. 9-12).

If the development of a microscopic sperm into a full-grown human child or the development of a small seed into a full-grown tree had not been taking place before our eyes, they are so wonderful a phenomenon that we could have hardly believed in their evolutionary character as we do with regard to the evolution of the solar system or the different species of animals. Then, when the Qur'an declares that nothing comes into existence without undergoing gradual development from a lower state to a higher state, why should it be believed that the human animal which appeared in its full physical perfection was an exception to this rule.

III. Gradual Process of Creation

In the verses quoted above in connection with the creation of man, it will be observed that the process of creation was gradual and not sudden. But from the words of the Qur'an, Kun, fa yakun," i.e., "Be, and it is," which occur very often in connection with the creation of things, it should not be understood that this happened in the twinkling of an eye.

The following verses are likely to be misunderstood.

(26) To Him is due the primeval origin of the heavens and the earth. When He decreeth a matter He sayeth to it Be, and it is (ii. 117).

(27) He created him [Adam] from dust; then He said to him Be, and he was (iii. 58).

As a matter of fact this phrase refers to two independent stages: Kun stands, so to say, for Amr (command) which is premeasurement and yakun for actual creation and completion. God decides on an Amr, or in their words, He commands it by saying Kun, i.e., Be. Thus if we postulate the primeval basis of existence, the cause of all causes, Kun is merely the commanding stage. It is a single thing unrelated to time. The next stage no doubt commences in the twinkling of an eye, as the Qur'an puts it:

(28) Surely We have created everything according to a measure, and Our command is but one as the twinkling of an eye (liv. 45-50).

There is no interposition of time or condition between the Will and its consequence, for with the command the process of creation starts to which the term *khalaqa* is to be applied.

(29) Surely your Lord is Allah Who created (*Khalaqa*) the heavens and the earth in six periods of time (vii. 54).

(30) Surely your Lord is Allah Who created (*Khalaqa*) the heavens and the earth in six periods (x. 3).

(31) And He it is Who created (*Khalaqa*) the heavens and the earth in six periods (xi. 17).

This again involves the idea of measuring and fitting into a scheme already ordained. It means that function of creation in case of man, which is laid down in the Qur'an itself, that is the function whereby the germ holds, and gradually becomes a clot, flesh, and bones, and then takes the shape of man as we have noted in quotation No. 17 (xxiii. 12-14).

Thus with *Kun* the process of creation starts at once, but it does not mean that it is completed immediately. The Qur'an speaks of the creation of the heavens and the earth in six periods or stages as we have noted in quotation No. 29 (vii. 54). Even if the word *Yaum* is translated as day, it cannot be understood as immediate, yet "*Kun, fa yakun*" has been rightly applied to their creation as we have noted in quotation No. 26 (ii. 117), for immediately with the command the creation started and became completed in due course of time appointed by God.

IV. The Six Stages of Creation

Similarly, in the creation of all that we find on the earth six stages are counted. The geologists and the biologists fix them in this way. The first stage commences from the time when the earth was thrown out of the molten mass of matter, the sun, and continued through the long period that it must have taken to cool down to an equable temperature and become fit for life to grow thereon. The second stage began when the earth became fit for organic life and it must have covered several millions of years. The third stage was then set for animal life and who knows how long did it take before the first germ of life, now called protoplasm, could emerge and how long it took to mould a body for itself and carry it forward from a lower form to a higher form until the fourth stage was reached when all kinds of animal life came into being.

In the fifth stage some of this animal life began to assume its present human shape on the physical plane and it must have takes millions of years to prepare him to acquire the requisite intellect before man could take his station on the cultural plane in the sixth stage at which man came into being which is no other than the Adam of the Qur'an. We shall not be wrong if we assert that all that has been wrought since the formation of the earth is but one long story of man's growth and development. The Qur'an is not silent in this respect also. It says:

(32) And indeed He has created you through various conditions (lxxi. 14).

Which implies that man has been brought to the present state of physical perfection after passing through various conditions. The Qur'an, therefore, calls him as the sign of God in these words:

(33) And one of His signs is that He created you from dust, then, lo! you are mortals who scatter (xxx. 30).

Indeed man's evolution from mere dust or clay which is the physical basis of his body, then out of the produce of the earth as incorporated in the parents' body, the production of the sperm-drop with the corresponding receptive element and then mixing of the different elements in due proportion and giving a particular shape and fashioning him into a man, then the breathing into him of the Spirit of God, giving him a mind and soul by which he can almost compass the farthest reaches of time and space--is not all this enough for a miracle or sign?

These stages of man's physical growth from nothing till he completes the cycle of this life are described in the Qur'an in words whose accuracy, beauty, and comprehensiveness can only be fully appreciated by biologists.

V. The Six Spiritual Stages of Man's Growth

Parallel to this physical growth it is pointed out that man's spiritual growth is again brought to perfection in six stages.

(a) The *Ammarah*--the commanding stage which is the nascent condition of the self in the garb of bestial passions where animal impulses predominate. These are hardly controllable and tend to iniquity.

(34) Most surely man's self is wont to command him to do evil (xii. 53).

(*b*) The *Lawwamah*--the self-accusing or the upbraiding spirit which feels conscious of evil and resists it, asks for God's grace and pardon with repentance. The disciplinary courses prescribed by Islam are intended to produce this spirit which is called Conscience which helps man to practise all virtue and shun all evil.

(35) I call to witness the self-reproaching spirit (lxxv. 2).

(*c*) The *Mulhimah*--the inspired. That is the stage where inspiration comes and brings the soul on the road to perfection when temptations die and cravings for virtue increase.

(36) In the case of those who say, Our Lord is Allah and stand steadfast, the angels descend on them and say: Fear not, nor grieve, and receive the glad tidings of the garden of bliss which you are promised (xli. 30).

(*d*) The *Mutma'innah*--the spirit at peace, where evil disappear and virtue becomes man's food and the soul begins to rule the flesh.

(37) Allah has endeared the faith to you and has made it beautiful in your hearts and He has made hateful to you unbelief, wickedness and transgression. Such indeed are those who walk in righteousness, a grace and favour from Allah, and Allah is full of knowledge and wisdom (xlix. 7-8).

(*e*) and (*f*) The *Radiyah* and *Mardiyah*--pleased with and pleasing God. These are the fifth and sixth evolutionary stages of our soul. Thus we teach the door of heaven on this very earth.

(38) Thou soul at rest, return to thy Lord, pleased with Him and He pleased with thee, enter among My servants and enter into My Paradise (lxxxix. 27-30).

Thus man's soul reaches its zenith and the spirit of God breathed in him, as the perfection of his physical frame brings him to spiritual perfection. We reach the final stage and the angels of God, the movers of the forces of nature, fall prostrate to our will.

This is the story of man beginning with dust and reaching to the exalted office of the vicegerent of God on earth. In other words, man's consciousness which was the result of God's breathing of His spirit into him at his physical perfection evolved from self-consciousness to cosmic consciousness manifesting Divine attributes, and this is the highest goal of human consciousness.

To understand the true significance of the story of Adam and his conflict with Satan as given in the Qur'an, we must bear in mind that the aim of the Qur'an is to guide man in the selection of his life's objective and show him who should be the object of his devotion and why should he seek His pleasure and by what ways and means His pleasure may be secured. For the achievement of this purpose the Qur'an does not burden the mind with philosophic speculations but impresses the truth by way of parables and allegories in a dramatic style. In this mode of expression the truth is presented to the mind in a picturesque manner and notwithstanding the brevity of words it helps to impress the mind with what it wants to impress in a realistic way.

For instance, to show that in the very nature of man there is a quest to find God and that his devotion to Him and submission to His will is the very essence of his nature, the Qur'an has told it in a graphic manner in the form of a parable.

(39) When thy Lord brought forth from the children of Adam from their loins their descendants and made them bear witness against themselves: Am I not your Lord? They said: Yea! We bear witness. Lest you should say on the Day of Resurrection: Surely we were unformed of this (vii. 172).

This verse does not narrate any event that took place in the annals of mankind but it only expresses an eternal truth which is the inner voice of our own self which calls us towards God. The same truth is expressed in the Qur'an in other places in these words:

(40) And in their souls (too are the signs of Allah). Will you not then reflect? (li. 21).

(41) Nay! man is evidence against himself though he puts forth excuses (lxxv. 14-15).

Another example of this mode of expression can be seen in the following verse:

(42) Surely We offered the trust to the heavens and the earth and the mountains but they refused to bear it and feared from it but man bore it. Indeed he is unjust and ignorant (xxxiii. 72).

From this it is intended to show that the urge to gain Divine love is a special gift of God given to man and to no other being but this carries with it great responsibilities, for it may take a wrong course easily in diverse manner. Man should consider it as a sacred trust and make use of it in the right direction and should not use it in devotion to objects other than God. If he does not realise his responsibility which he often does and fails to discharge it properly, he is deprived of that eminence which God has given him on this account over all of His creatures.

There are several instances bringing out this idea in the Qur'an. The story of Adam illustrates the struggle which man has to make to overcome the forces of Evil in order that he may be raised to that spiritual eminence which is the attainable end of his existence. Let us now study the story of Adam as presented by the Qur'an.

VI. The Parable of Adam

(43) And when thy Lord said to the angels: I am going to appoint in the earth a vicegerent, they said: Wilt Thou place therein one who will make mischief and shed blood, whilst we celebrate Thy praise and glorify Thy holy name? He said: Surely I know what you do not know. And He taught Adam the names of all things, then presenting them to the angels He said: Tell Me the names of these if you are right. They said: Glory be to Thee, we have no knowledge except what Thou hast taught us, surely Thou art the Knowing, the Wise.

He said: O Adam! tell them their names. Then when he had told them their names, He said: Did I not tell you that I know the secrets of the heavens and the earth, and that I know what you reveal and what you conceal.

And when We said to the angels: May obeisance to Adam, they did obeisance, not so Iblis: he refused and was haughty and he was of the rejectors (ii. 30-34).

VII. Adam's Position in the Scheme of Creation

The first verse of this passage defines our position on earth. The former revelations spoke of man as being made after the image of God. This was vague and could therefore be diversely interpreted, but the Qur'an tells us that we have come here as lords of the creation to rule upon the earth in the capacity of vicegerents of God. We have not only been given essential capacities but also the aptitude to learn all that is necessary for

knowing and utilising the various resources of nature and the
sentient begins called angels who bring the powers of nature into
operation have also been made subject to us.

It is apparent that everything happening in the universe comes
from God, but His Will manifests itself through other agencies
created by Him in the various manifestations of Nature. These in
themselves possess no intelligence but their work is marvelously
regular and of mathematical exactitude in every way, so much so
that we are almost compelled to believe that they do possess a
mind. The angels act as mind in these unintelligent things enabling
them to display their properties when required.

These verses refer to a controversy between God and in angels
as to the propriety of His creating a creature like man on the earth
who would make mischief in it. A dispute like this could not
possibly occur between God and His angels as they are of a
ministerial nature. They have to obey orders, so they could not
find fault with the work of the Lord. When we consider human
nature and study and the universe around us, it appears to be
without flaw or imperfection. Beauty and utility are its main
features, but it is a man who sets himself to abuse these gifts of
God and create mischief. We naturally wonder why the Lord of
perfection and beauty created such a pestilent creature like man
to encumber the earth. If He wanted to give expression to His own
nature, which is above all evil and flaw, the work of the angels
was sufficient for it. This objection often arises in the human mind,
and here it has been put into the mougth of the angels. The Arabic
words *Tasbih* and *Hamd* stand for God's freedom from all
imperfections and the possession of all praiseworthy attributes. The
claim put forth by the angels therefore means that He is not only
above all error and evil but that He possesses all good qualities.
Everything in nature in its existing form bears strong testimony
to this, but nature contains a world of potentialities which on their
actualisation will bear witness to the further glorification and purity
of the Lord. It is left to man to bring those capacities of nature
to fruition. Hence his creation was necessary. The angels were
unable to understand the need for the creation of man and they
asked God concerning it and He told them: "Surely I know what
you do not know."

By way of illustration let us take electricity. It must be the work of angels to make it in the form in which it exists. It is free from any error in its make-up and manifests accurately the character given to it but it is man and not any angel who has put electricity to such wonderful uses. So the Lord replies that He knows the work which man has to do in order to establish Divine glory and His freedom from all imperfections Man, of course, will make mistakes. He has risen from the animal and still inherits animal passions. But he has guidance, he may or may not make a wrong use of these passions since evil is after all only a mis-application of a thing good in itself. Hence the objection raised by the angels. But the very knowledge that man has the aptitude to acquire will also enable him to curb his animal inclinations, if he so wills. This superiority of man over the angels lies in his ability to acquire the knowledge of properties of things and of turning them to his advantage which is not possessed by the angels.

Unless, therefore, man acquires that knowledge and puts it to its proper use, he is not true to himself. His every creation has been justified solely because of the said knowledge. We must therefore acquire knowledge of everything including our moral and spiritual natures. Then only we shall be the vicegerents of God on this earth.

VIII. Iblis- the Power of Evil, a Moral Necessity

Next we read of another being called Iblis--Satan. He by his nature belongs to such an order of creation as under the law of contrast will go against everything else. If angels declare their willingness to obey man Satan must needs refuge to do so, just as toxins or poisons are introduced into our body to make the while cells of our blood become active to increase vitality and improve our health and make them immune to outside infections; so also we need some poison on the moral plane to make us immune from sin. If the body gives rise to a spirit in our system whose health depends on the exercise of good morals, some evil spirit is surely needed to remove all sluggishness from it. The Evil one has been called Satan in religious phraseology. We do need him. He must work on wrong lines to keep the spirit of goodness ever active. Satan ranks on the moral plane with the toxins of physical plane. We find in the Qur'an the same functions assigned to him as are allotted to toxins in the physical kingdom. Like them he introduces himself within us from outside. He acts as enemy and weakens our sense of morality and tries to destroy it. But if we make our moral nature assert itself strongly enough, by following the laws of God, we become immune from all sin. The Devil then, like toxins, subserves a moral end. The two poisons, toxins and Satan, assail our health and spirit on identical lines. Evil works on the same lines as those adopted by Satan according to the description in the Qur'an. They are indeed one and the same. Is it the perversity of our own mind that we call Satan, or is it some personality existent in the external world who invites the mind to evil? In other words, is Satan a mere faculty or a being who inspires us to use our faculties for evil?

He cannot be a part of our physical nature. If good morals depend upon the activity of the good Spirit there must also be some evil Spirit also be energies it to the full extent possible. Satan must be the Evil Spirit. Is he an external entity or something from within that causes evil promptings? Inspiration, good or evil, has in it nothing of a physical nature. It is a kind of knowledge and no knowledge is born within us. It always comes from the outer world and we receive all inspiration from things external. So it must be that the Arch-fiend, the inspirer of evil is really an external agent. The story continues:

(44) Allah said: What prevented thee from making obeisance when I commanded thee? He said: I am better than he. Thou created me of fire and him of clay (vii. 12).

(45) He said: O Iblis What excuse has thou that thou art not with those who make obeisance. He said: I am not such that I should make obeisance to a mortal whom Thou hast created of the essence of black mud fashioned in shape (xv. 32-33).

(46) He [Iblis] said: Shall I make obeisance to him whom Thou hast created of dust; seest Thou? This is the one whom Thou hast honoured above me! (xvii 61).

(47) Allah said: Get forth from it. It does not befit thee to be arrogant here. Get out, for thou art of the object ones (vii. 13).

(48) He said: Then get out of it; surely thou art cast off and surely on thee is curse until the day of judgement (xv. 34-35).

Iblis not only refused to bow down, he refused to be of those who bowed down. In other words, he arrogantly despised the angels who bowed down as well as man to whom they bowed down and he was in rebellion against God by not obeying His order. Arrogance, jealously, and rebellion were his triple crime. Notice also the subtle viles of Iblis, his egotism in putting himself above man and his falsehood in ignoring the fact that God had not merely made man's body with the extract of clay (the word *Bashar* or mortal is used for man suggesting a gross physical (body) but had given him spiritual form and gave him the faculty of knowing things which raised him above the angels.

IX. The Challenge of Iblis

(49) He [Iblis] said: Give me respite till the day they are raised up. Allah said: Be thou among those who are given respite. He [Iblis] said: Because Thou hast thrown me out of the way, I will certainly lie in wait for them on Thy straight path. Then I will assault them from before them and behind them, from their right and their left, nor wilt Thou find most of them thankful. Allah said: Get out from this, disgraced and expelled. Whoever of them will follow thee, I will fill Hell with you all (vii. 14-18).

(50) [Iblis] said: O my Lord! Because Thou hast made life evil to me, I will certainly make evil fair-seeming to them on earth and I will certainly put them all in the wrong except. Thy servant among them sincere and purified by Thy grace. Allah said: This (way of My servants) is indeed the way that leads straight to Me and surely on My servants thou shalt have no authority except those who follow thee of the deviators and surely Hell is the promised place of them all (xv. 39-43).

(51) [Iblis] said: If thou wilt but respite me to the day of judgement I will surely bring his descendants under my sway--all but a few. Allah said: Go thy way. If anyone follow thee verily Hell will be the recompense of you all-an ample recompense. Lead to destruction those whom thou canst among them, with thy seductive voice make assaults on them with thy cavalry and thy infantry, mutually share with them wealth and children, and make

promises to them--but Satan promises them nothing but deceit. As for My servants, no authority shalt thou have over them. Enough is thy Lord for a Disposer of affairs. (xvii. 62-65).

In the conversation given in the above verses between God and Iblis (Satan) the use of plural for man shows that it is the story of all men struggling constantly with the power of evil that is being metaphorically described here, and that Adam and mankind are synonymous terms.

The assault of evil is depicted here as coming from all sides. It takes advantage of every weak point and sometimes even our good and generous sympathies are used to decoy us into the snares of evil.

Man has every reason to be grateful to God for all His loving care, and yet man in his folly forgets his gratitude and does the very opposite of what he should do. The grip of evil continues only as long as man is not spiritually raised. Satan's demand of respite is only till the time of man's spiritual resurrection. In God's grant of free-will to man is implied the faculty of choosing between good and evil and this faculty is exercised through the temptations and allurements put forward by Satan. This is the period of man's probation on earth. Even so, no temptations have power over the sincere devotees of God, who are purified by His grace. This purification changes the whole nature of man. After that evil is powerless to touch him.

Apart from such purified souls everyone who worships God invites God's grace to protect him. But if he puts himself in the way of wrong and deliberately chooses evil, the responsibility falls upon the sinner himself who puts himself into Satan's power.

Evil has many snares for mankind. The one that is put in the foreground is the voice--the seductive personal appeal that makes worse appear better. Next comes force when cajolery and tempting and fair-seeming fails. If the first assault is resisted, evil has other weapons in its armoury. Tangible fruits like ill-gotten gains and ill-gotten children or the carnal pleasures out of fornication and adultery and similar alluring methods of indulgence in animal passions are dangled before the eyes. But all the promises of the Evil One are worth nothing and only lead to destruction. In all this controversy, one point is made very clear and that is that evil has no power except over those who yield to its solicitations.

X. The Trial of Adam

(52) And We said: O Adam! Dwell thou and thy wife in the garden and eat of the bountiful things therein as you both wish, but do not approach this tree, otherwise you both will be of those who commit injustice to themselves. (ii. 35).

(53) Then We said: O Adam! Verily this Iblis is an enemy to thee and thy wife; so, let him not get you both out of the garden so that you are landed in misery. There is therein enough provision for thee not to go hungry nor to go naked, nor to suffer from thirst, nor from the heat of the sun.

But Satan whispered evil to him; he said: O Adam! Shall I lead thee to the tree of eternity and to a kingdom that never decays? (xx. 117-120)

(54) The Satan began to whisper suggestions to them that he might manifest to them what was unnoticed by them of their private parts. He said: Your Lord only forbade you this tree lest you should become angels or such beings as live for ever. And he swore to them both that he was their sincere adviser. So he beguiled them by deceit.

When they both tasted of the tree, their private parts became manifest to each other and they both began to cover themselves with the leaves of the garden; and their Lord called on to them: Did I not forbid you both from that tree and tell you that Satan was your avowed enemy? They said: Our Lord! we have wronged ourselves. If Thou forgive us not and bestow not upon us Thy mercy, we shall certainly be of those who cause loss to themselves. (vii. 20-23).

(55) And We had beforehand made a covenants with Adam, but he forgot and We found on his part no firm resolve. (xx. 115).

(56) When they both ate of it their private parts became manifest to them both and they began to cover themselves with the leaves of the garden. Thus Adam disobeyed his Lord and allowed himself to be seduced. (xv. 121).

(57) But Satan caused them to deflect therefrom and expelled
them from the state in which they were. (ii. 36).

Before we understand the true significance of the verses quoted
above, there are two things which are to be determined first. One
is the word *Jannat* or the garden and the other is *Shajarah*, the
forbidden tree.

God began the creation of man (Adam) from dust (xxxii, 7) a
part of the earth only and after the various cycles of existence
through which this dust hud to pass, man, the intellectual man,
endowed with the capacity to acquire knowledge and possessed
with a free-will to discriminate between good and evil, was
evolved, and was placed on the earth as a vicegerent of God, and
all those beings which operated the forces of nature (the angels)
were made subservient to him. At the same time he was warned
of the power of evil and ordered to keep out of its way.

Therefore there is no ground to believe that the "Garden" he
and his wife were asked to stay in, was Paradise, as commonly
understood. The Paradise which is described in the Qur'an in
metaphorical terms is a state of bliss, a closeness to the very
presence of the Divine Being, attained by the righteous in life-after-
death as a recompense of their good deeds done in their
probationary life on earth. There is no question of Satan or evil
entering into this state of bliss and tempting its inmates, as is
envisaged in the story of Adam.

The "Garden" mentioned in the story of Adam signifies a state
of ease and comfort, free of difficulties and troubles, where food
is available without exertion and where Adam and his wife shall
not be hungry, nor thirsty, nor bare of clothing nor feel the heat
of the sun (xx. 120), and the warning given was: "Let him (Satan)
not get you both out of the garden, so that you are landed in
misery." (xx. 117) All this shows that life in the garden meant a
state of comfort, ease, contentment and happiness, in which there
was no struggle or distress on this very earth itself. Satan as
mentioned in ii, 36 "caused them to deflect there from and expelled
them from the *state* in which they were". So it is clear from these
verses that this state of felicity which Adam and his mate enjoyed
in their life was on earth only before their succumbing to the
temptation of Satan.

XI. The Significance of the Shajarah

Now the word *Shajarah* as it has occurred in the context of the garden is generally translated as tree but it bears a different significance when considered in the light of the temptation offered and its consequent result depicted. Every time it is mentioned the words used are, "Do not approach this tree "or" Do not go near this tree" -(ii. 35 and vii. 19). How can going near a tree or approaching a tree constitute an offence? If it was meant eating the fruit .of a particular tree, there are no words to suggest this meaning. On the other hand, in all the sentences which refer to this incident it is said:

(*a*) Your Lord forbade you this tree. (vii. 20)

(*b*) When they tasted the tree. (xii. 22).

(*c*) When they both ate of it. (xx. 121).

(*d*) Did I not forbid you from that tree? (vii. 22)

No one tastes a tree or eats a tree and the Qur'an which is an eloquent piece of literature is least expected to use such ambiguous 'expressions if it meant only the eating or tasting the fruits of the tree.

The words "Do not go near" are used in the Qur'an elsewhere in a different context.:

(58) Do not go nigh to fornication. (vii. 32).

(59) Do not draw nigh to indecencies. (vi. 152)

(60) Do not go near them (your wives) until they have become clean. (ii. 222)

(61) Do not go near them (your wives) while you keep to the mosques. (ii. 187)

In all these verses the Qur'an not only forbids fornication or indecencies, or sexual intercourse with one's own wives when they are in monthly courses, but enjoins upon men not to go near them thus avoiding even all those opportunities which are likly to tempt one to commit them.

If the word *Shajarah* was meant to be a tree whose fruit was forbidden, command would have been not to eat its fruit and not "Not to go near it".

Again in the verse "When they tasted the tree" (vii. 22) the word "tasting" is used in the Qur'an not in the sense of eating as can be seen from the following verses:

(62) They shall not *taste* therein death. (xliv. 57)

(63) Then pour above his head of the torment of the boiling water: *taste* thereof . (xliv. 48).

(64) They shall not *taste* therein cold. (lxxviii. 24).

(65) So *taste:* for We will not add to you aught but chastisement.

(66) *Taste* the abiding chastisement for what you did. (xxxiv. 42)

(67) *Taste* the chastisement of fire which you called a lie (xxxiv. 42).

(68) Allah made it to *taste* the utmost degree of hunger and fear because of what they wrought. (xvi. 42)

From the above verses it will be seen that the word "taste" is used in connection with many kinds of experiences quite apart from eating with the mouth.

Again to emphasise that the word *Shajarah* is not used in the meaning of a tree, it is said: "They both began to cover themselves with the leaves of the *garden*". (vii. 22) Here the word *Shajarah* (tree) is avoided and in its place "garden" is used so that the meaning of the word *Shajarah* which is used a few words earlier in a different sense may not be confused with a tree the leave of which they sought to cover their nakedness.

So, it will be abundantly clear now that the word *Shajarah* does not stand for a tree in the verses describing the story of Adam.

Then what does it stand for, is a point to consider here. The key to understand its true significance is made available to us in the words used by Satan and the result it produced on Adam and his wife on tasting it. Mark the words used by Satan:

On Adam! Shall I lead thee to the tree of eternity and to a kingdom that never decays. (xxx 120)

The Satan whispered suggestions to them that he might manifest to them what was unnoticed by them of their private parts. He said: Your Lord only forbade you this tree that you should become two angels or such being as live for ever. (vii. 20).

It is only through the progeny of Adam, the result of the union of the sexes, that the race of mankind attains a perpetual existence. The function of the private parts was not known to the pair until Satan whispered suggestions to them about their use. The word "whisper" is very suggestive indicating that the sexual urge is first both within and reaches its consummation by the stimulation it receives from outside environments. This urge received its impetus from the suggestions given by Satan with the result that the union of the sexes took place. This is expressed in the Qur'an in these words: "when they both tasted of the tree their private parts became manifest to each other and they both began to cover themselves with the leaves of the garden." (vii. 22)

It was after the commission of the sexual act that the consciousness of their nakedness dawned upon them and "they both began to cover themselves with the leaves of the garden."

Thus it will be seen that the forbidden tree is no other than the sexual act and God took a covenant from Adam that he would not indulge in it before he was permitted to do so as is given in verse xx. 115: "And We had beforehand made a covenant with Adam but he forgot and We found on his part no firm resolve".

This is what generally happens, when opposite sexes lives together and that is why in verses xvii 32. vi. 152, ii. 187 and ii. 222 quoted above, the words "do not draw nigh or go near" are used so that all opportunities of temptations, however remote they might be, could be avoided. It was a trial in which Adam was placed to demonstrate the fact that however man may be equipped with wisdom and knowledge, he cannot of himself find the way to rectitude without guidance from God, and this guidance, we are told, was provided to them as stated in the verse:

(69) Then Adam received words from his Lord and so He turned to him mercifully. Surely, He is oft-returning to mercy, the Merciful. (ii. 37)

and the repentance of Adam is recorded in these words:

They said: Our Lord! We have wronged ourselves. If Thou forgive us not and bestow not Thy mercy on us, we shall certainly be of those who cause loss to themselves (vii. 23).

The word "tree" is used for the sexual act because just as a seed when planted in the soil gradually assumes its stature as a full-grown tree and produces in its turn millions of seeds to propagate the species, a similar process takes place for the propagation of the human species by the sexual act. That is why the genealogy of man is represented in the from of a tree and on this account only the word *Shajarah* is used for the genealogy of man in the Arabic tongue. The Qur'an also compares the creation

of man with the creation of a tree in these words:
(70) And Allah has made you grow out of the earth in the
manner of a plant. (lxxi. 18)
The Qur'an contains directions for the physical as well as the
moral and spiritual welfare of man and it deals with the most
delicate problems in a language unapproached in its purity by any
other law dealing with similar subjects. It is a miracle of the Qur'an
that while it was produced in the language of a people whose poets
took pride in describing the relations of the sexes in the most
indecent words and phrases, the language of the Qur'an is
unsurpassed in purity and decency when dealing with the delicate
relations of the sexes so much so, that even the most modest reader
of the Qur'an need have no shudder while reciting it. It is,
therefore, perfectly in accordance with this principle that the
Qur'an calls the sexual act by the word *Shajarah* and commands
both Adam and his mate not to go near it. It was indeed a trial
for both of them and they could not keep their covenant with God.
The sexual urge from within and the seductive encouragement
given by the powers of evil from without shook his resolve.
--"And We found on his part on firm resolve." (xx. 11).

XII. Adam's Ultimate Destiny

Adam had been given the will to choose and he chose to
disobey, but it was not deliberately done. God's grace came to his
aid when he was about to be lost in the throng of the evil ones.
His repentance was accepted and God chose him for His mercy.
(71) But his Lord chose him (for His grace). He turned to him
and gave him guidance. (xx. 122)
But he could not now enjoy that facility and freedom from all
the worries of life after once taking to the family life and therefore
they both had to quit the garden to bliss in which they were placed
to carry on a struggle with the devil that is their enemy.
(72) We said: Get forth, fome of you being the enemies of the
other and there is for you in the earth an abode and a
provision for a time. (ii. 36)
(73) He said: Get forth, you two, therefrom, all (of you) with
enmity one to another. (xx. 123).
The little variation in the above two passages is instructive.
The dual number refers to two individual souls, our common

ancestors, and the plural number includes all mankind and Satan, for the argument is about the collective life of man.

The new condition in which man is placed is the condition of mutual enmity. As opposed to the happy state of life it is one in which man has to face distress and difficulties. It is a state of life which the virtuous and the wicked must equally pass through. In fact, it is ónly trials and hardships of life that make perfection attainable. The first state of ease is not a state of perfection as in the child, though it may be a state of ease and comfort, but as man must attain to a state of perfection, he has to pass through the necessary trials. This is made clear in the verses that follow that all men have to follow Divine guidance if they wish to attain to a state of freedom from fear and grief which in the Qur'an always represent the goal of life or the final state of perfection as far as the life on this earth is concerned.

(74) We said: Go forth from this state all; so surely there will come to you guidance from Me; then whosoever follows My guidance, no fear shall come upon them nor shall they grieve. And as to those who choose disbelief and belie our messages, they shall be the inmates of fire and in it they shall abide. (ii. 38-39)

(75) He said: Get forth you two therefrom, all (of you) with enmity one to another. But if there come to you guidance from Me, then whosoever follows My guidance will not go astray nor fall into distress; but whosoever turns away from My message, verily for him is a straitened life and We shall raise him up blind on the day of judgment. (xx. 123-124).

The consequences of following the guidance of God are twofold. They will be saved from going astray and on them shall be no fear nor shall they grieve; and the consequences of rejecting God's guidance which shall be made available to man through God's prophets will be a straitened life, a life of spiritual blindness both in this life and its continuation after death.

The whole story of Adam unfolds a lesson--the greatest of all spiritual lessons--how to conquer evil and how to subdue the animal passions to be able to rise to the greatest spiritual heights for which man is created until he reaches the stage when God would say:

(76) Thou soul at rest! Return to Thy Lord, pleased with Him
and He pleased with thee; enter among My servants and
enter into My Paradise. (lxxxix. 27-30)

The story of Adam as narrated by the Qur'an is the story of
man, giving a picture of human nature. It does say indeed that
he was made from dust but then it as well speaks of every son
of man being created from dust. It speaks of the spirit of God which
stands for the soul being breathed into every man to enable him
to distinguish between right and wrong.

It refers to the high place he is intended to occupy on earth,
ruling not only the animal creation but the very force of nature
with the knowledge which he acquires through his efforts by slow
degrees. But that is not enough for him. It may lead him into the
clutches of Satan. To strengthen him further the light of the Divine
Spirit is available to him and by the use of that light he can rise
to higher and higher eminences. And just as in the physical world,
the acquirement of knowledge opens out new fields of advance-
ments before him, so in the spiritual world the knowledge of things
Divine opens out before him a higher life which will be fully
manifest in the life after death.

XIII. The Bible Story of Adam

It is claimed by Christian scholars that the Qur'an has borrowed
the story of Adam from the Bible. There may be a few similarities
in both the stories but that is not evidence enough to prove that
one is borrowed from the other. On the other hand, there are
several dissimilarities on vital points of the story which make the
one very different from the other. We have studied already what
the Qur'an has said in this connection. Let us now see what the
Bible says so that our readers may be able to judge for themselves
whether the Qur'an is indebted in any way to the story of the Bible.

(1) And the Lord God formed man of the dust of the ground
and breathed into his nostrils the breath of life; and man
became a living soul.

(2) And the Lord God planted a garden...and there he put the
man whom he had formed.

(3) And out of the ground made the Lord God... the tree of
life... and the tree of knowledge of good and evil.

(4) And the Lord God took the man, and put him into the
garden of Eden to dress it and to keep it.

(5) And the Lord commanded man, saying, Of every tree of the garden thou mayest freely eat: but of the tree of the knowledge of good and evil, thou shalt not eat of it: for in the day that thou eatest thereof thou shalt surely die.

(6) And the Lord God caused a deep sleep to fall upon Adam, and he slept: and he took one of his ribs, and closed up the flesh instead thereof; and the rib, which the Lord God had taken from man, made he a woman, and brought her unto the man.

(7) And they were both naked, the man and his wife, and they were not ashamed.

(8) ....And he (the serpent) said unto the woman, Yea, hath God said, Ye shall not eat of every tree of the garden? And the woman said unto the serpent, We may eat of the fruit of the trees of the garden: but of the fruit of the tree which is in the midst of the garden, God hath said, Ye shall not eat of it, neither shall ye touch it, lest ye die. And the serpent said unto the woman, Ye shall not surely die: for God doth know that in the day ye eat thereof, then your eyes shall be opened, and ye shall be as gods, knowing good and evil.

(9) And when the woman saw that the tree was good for food, and that is was pleasant to the eyes, and a tree to be desired to make one wise, she took of the fruit thereof and did eat, and gave also unto her husband with her; and he did eat. And the eyes of them both were opened, and they knew that they were naked; and they sewed fig leaves together, and made themselves aprons.

(10) And they heard the voice of the Lord God walking in the garden in the cool of the day: Adam and his wife hid themselves from the presence of their Lord God amongst the trees of the garden.

(11) And the Lord God called unto Adam, and said unto him, Where art thou? and he said: I heard thy voice in the garden, and I was afraid, because I was naked; and I hid myself. And he said, Who told thee that thou was naked? Hast thou eaten of the tree, whereof I commanded thee that thou shouldest not eat?

(12) And the man said, The woman whom thou gavest to be with me, she gave me of the tree and I did eat. And the Lord God said unto the woman. What is this that thou

hast done? and the woman said, The serpent beguiled me, and I did eat.

(13) And the Lord God said unto the serpent, Because thou has done this, thou art cursed above all cattle, and above every beast of the filed; upon thy belly shall thou go, and dust shalt thou eat all the days of thy life: and I will put enmity between thee and the woman, and between his seed and her seed; it shall bruise thy head, and thou shall bruise his heel.

(14) Unto the woman he said, I will greatly multiply thy sorrow and thy conception; in sorrow thou shalt bring forth children; and thy desire shall be to thy husband, and he shall rule over thee.

(15) And unto Adam he said, Because thou hast hearkened unto the voice of thy wife, and hast eaten of the tree, of which I commanded thee, saying, Thou shalt not eat of it: cursed is the ground for thy sake; in sorrow shalt thou eat of it all the days of thy life; thorns also and thistles shall it bring froth to thee; and thou shall eat the herb of the field. In the sweat of thy face shalt thou eat thy bread, till thou return unto the ground; for out of it wast thou taken: for dust thou art, and to dust shalt thou return.

(16) And Adam called his wife's name Eve; because she was the mother of all living.

(17) Unto Adam and also to his wife did the Lord God make coast of skin, and clothed them. And the Lord God said, Behold, the man is become one of us, to know good and evil, and now, lest he put forth his hand, and take also the tree of life, and eat, and live for ever: therefore the Lord God sent him forth from the garden of Eden, to till the ground from whence he was taken.

(18) So he drove out the man; and he placed at the east of the garden of Eden Cherubims, and a flaming sword which turned every way, to keep the way of the tree of life.

XIV. The Implications of the Bible Story

We have quoted above the very words of the Bible pertaining to the story of Adam. It will be noted that in the story as told in the Bible there is no mention of a "Fall". That term was manufactured afterwards in orthodox Christian theology. This must have originated in the literature of Babylon and was appropriated by Jewish writers after the Captivity. For, it was in Babylonian and Persian theology that the dualism existed of God and the Enemy or Evil Spirit in the form of a serpent.

Of course the story cannot be taken as real history. No one can read it intelligently and believe that what it describes actually happened. As history it is quite incredible.

To begin with man's body was shaped out of the dust of the ground and God breathed into his nostrils the breath of life and man became a living soul, an act of jugglery so to say, but to create the woman God had to take one of the ribs of Adam. He was heard walking in the garden and man and woman tried to hide themselves from God Who knew not where they were and called out "where art thou?" God cursed the serpent and made it crawl as a punishment though serpent never walked upright. God cursed the ground by making it bring forth thorns and thistles though thorns and thistles came from the ground before man existed on the earth.

God is afraid of man knowing too much and expels the man and the woman from the garden to prevent them from eating of the tree of life which would give them immortality, though nothing could make a fleshly body immortal. God is represented here to be like a man--jealous, changeable, revengeful, threatening a death penalty for committing the offence of eating the fruit of the tree of knowledge which was not executed when the command was disobeyed. He appears as if He is afraid of the growing power of'the creature He had himself made, and calls upon supernatural powers with swords of flame to bar his way to the tree of life.

The man and the woman were only seeking knowledge. To know the difference between good and evil is necessary for any progress or improvement and there was nothing discreditable in the woman's conduct not in that of the man. In fact man's superiority over all other creatures of the earth is due to his knowledge and the will to put that knowledge into proper use and rule the earth.

God cursed man for his disobedience by making him earn his bread by the sweat of his face. The doctrine that work is a curse cannot be accepted. It is man's greatest or one of his greatest blessings. Without work man cannot life.

Work is not a curse of itself or in itself, but only when it is evil work or when it is slavery and made an end in itself and not a means to the tailor's betterment.

God cursed the woman to conceive in sorrow and to bring forth children in sorrow. This again is not true to human nature. The sexual act which is the genesis of conception is a pleasure which both the sexes enjoy and the pains of labour that the woman is subjected to at the moment of child-birth are not pains of sorrow. They are pains which the mother willingly suffers to enjoy the pleasures of motherhood later on. Motherhood is not a curse but a boon conferred by God on the womenfolk. The whole story is a cunningly devised fable of preistcraft. Jesus called the Old Testament as traditions of the elders and denounced it. It is a pity that Hebrew and Christian theology has become a fable built upon the doctrine of the "Fall of Man".

II

THE STORY OF THE PROPHET NUH (NOAH)
(May peace and blessings of God be on him)

Rain and Revelation Compared

Before we read the stories of the prophets as narrated by the Qur'an, it may be noted that the Qur'an makes use of a beautiful simile of rain and its effect on the land to impress the real import of Divine revelation. The simile runs as follows:

(1) He (Allah) it is Who sendeth forth the winds spreading abroad the tidings of His blessings to follow till they bring up the laden clouds to move along to some dry spot of land, so as to pour down water thereon to cause therewith an upgrowth of all kinds of fruit. In like manner do We revive those who are lost to life is ye only can ponder. In a rich soil plants spring froth in abundance by the will of its Lord, and in that which is bad, they spring forth but scantily. Thus in varying ways do We make things clear for those who gratefully respond to Our call (vii. 57-58).

The revelation that is given to the prophets is here compared to rain by which the prophets raise a dead nation to life. Those whose talents have been lying dormant for lack of proper lead and guidance are awakened by it to activity and made advantageous use of them to get fully developed and profited by them. Those who are of an evil temperament create obstacles in their own way of taking advantage of it and deprive themselves of its blessings.

In every age on the advent of a prophet, humanity divided itself into two main sections, one prospering in every way with a receptive nature for all that is good, and the other falling into the abyss of moral and spiritual degradation with temperament repelling good and incined towards evil. The touchstone of ordeals exposed the worthlessness of half-hearted people, who being discarded by one or both of the male sections, were left to perish like the scum that is skimmed off by a goldsmith while purifying gold, and sometimes this same fate overtook the unbelieving section also.

I. The Advent of Noah

The history of the prophets commences with the story of Noah and his people. According to the Qur'an, after Adam the prophet, who had left his progeny in a state of social and moral health, it was sometime before the advent of Noah that human society began to show corruption and depravity, and, therefore, God sent Noah, His apostle, for their reclamation.

The people of Noah were dwelling in that part of the earth which is now called Iraq. Traditions similar to the story of the people of Noah are extant in the literature of various nations both in the East and the West, showing that the incident of the Deluge probable occurred in an epoch in which the progeny of Adam was still confined to one particular region of the earth and after the deluge they must have spread out and migrated to various parts of the earth. That seems to be the probable reason why every nation possesses some primitive record in the beginning of its history of a deluge, though its details have become obscured with the passage of time leaving behind only imaginary legends.

The people of Noah were not disbelievers in God but they associated other gods with God and the priests of these deities exercised great control over all religious, political and economic affairs of the country. Society had been split up into different sections and had given birth to corruption, oppression, and injustice, causing disruption in the collective life of the community. Moral depravity and turpitude had uprooted the very foundations of social structure. Noah had to work very strenuously for a very long time with patient preservance and tactfulness to bring about a reformation but the people were so stubborn under the influence of their priests that very little could be done by him until at last in sheer disgust he had to cry out: "My Lord! Leave not upon land any dweller from among the disbeliever." (lxxi. 96).

What happened between Noah and his people was similar to that which happened between Muhammad (may peace be on him) and his compatriots. The important facts about the Deluge are narrated to his opponents to point out that truth shall ultimately prevail and that opposition shall entirely fail and his enemies will finally be overthrown. The same is the aim of all similar narratives about the life incidents of all previous prophets.

It may be asked why such wholesale destruction of rebellious communities does not take place now-a-days. The fact is that when a prophet is sent to a nation and that nation rejects him, the threatened chastisement should deservedly descend on that nation so that evil may be rooted out and virtue rewarded. After the advent of the last Prophet Muhammad (may peace be on him) who succeeded in the establishment of a state based on Divinely revealed laws and regulations preserved for ever in the Book called the Qur'an, the situation has changed completely. But now calamities like war, famine, flood, etc., do afflict corrupt humanity on a large scale, but they are explained away by scientists, philosophers, statesmen and historians of the modern age who attribute these happenings to physical, geographical, political and historical causes and do not let the people think of God Who first chastises the iniquitous people by various ailments such as scarcity and famine, and when they persist in their iniquities paying no heed to His warnings, He makes them reap the fruits of their misdeeds in large-scale calamities.

II. Noah's Preachings

Let us now see what the Qur'an has to say about Noah and his people. We have already pointed out in the introduction that the Bible cannot claim to be the source of these stories as some of the Christian critics of the Qur'an have laboured to make the world believe, and therefore we have shown in footnotes the differences in both the narratives and left the judgment with the readers to distinguish which is mere folklore and which is the revealed communication of God.

(2) Certainly We sent Nuh to his people.[1] He said: O my people! Serve Allah: you have no god other than Him. If

---

1. The Qur'an speaks again and again of Noah being sent to a particular people and only of their destruction by the deluge. It may be noted here that the Qur'an does not support the theory of a world deluge, for it plainly states here that Noah was sent only to his people and not to all nations Only the people who rejected Noah were drowned. But according to the Bible the Deluge covered the whole earth and its result was destruction of all flesh on the surface of the earth.

you refuse surely I fear for you the chastisement of a grievous day.² The chiefs of his people replied: Most surely we perceive thee in clear error. He said: O my people! There is no error in me but I am an apostle from the Lord of the worlds. I deliver to you the message of my Lord and I counsel you right, and I know from Allah what you do not know. Do you wonder that an admonition has come to you from your Lord through a man from among you to warn you that you may take heed to yourselves and that haply mercy be shown to you.

But they accused him of imposture and so We delivered him and those who were with him in the ark and We drowned those who rejected Our communications. Surely they were a blind people. (vii. 59-64).

(3)   The people of Nuh rejected the apostle. When their brother Nuh said to them: Will you not guard against evil? Surely I am a faithful apostle to you. Therefore guard against the punishment of Allah and obey me. I do not ask of you any recompense for it. My reward is only with the Lord of the worlds. So, guard against the punishment of Allah and obey me.

They said: Shall we believe in thee while the meanest follow thee? He said: What knowledge have I of what they do? Their account is only with my Lord if you could

---

"And the waters prevailed exceedingly upon the earth; and all the high hills, that were under the whole heaven, were covered. Fifteen cubits upward did the waters prevail; and the mountains were covered And all flesh died that moved upon the earth, both of fowl and of cattle, and of beast, and of every creeping thing that creepeth upon the earth, and every man." (Genesis, 7; 19-21)

2. According to the Qur'an, the Deluge was a punishment only for the particular people who persisted in their evil ways and rejected the truth and refused to bow before God.

The Bible is silent about Noah's preachings to his people and his great struggle to bring about their reformation. It tells us only that there was wickedness in the whole of the earth while only Noah was a just man and perfect in his generations and that God told Noah to make an ark for himself and his family as He was going to destroy the earth and all on it.

perceive. I am not going to drive away the believers, for,
I am naught but a plain warner.

They said: If thou desist not, O Nuh! Thou shalt most
certainly be of those stoned to death.

He said: My Lord! Surely my people take me for a liar.
Therefore judge Thou between me and between them with
a just judgement, and deliver me and those who are with
me of the believers. (xxvi. 105-118).

(4) Recite to them the story of Nuh when he said to his people:
O my people! If my stay and my reminding you by
Allah's communications is hard on you--yet on Allah do
I rely--then make your designs against me and gather your
associates and let not your course of action be in doubt
for you; then have it executed against me and give me no
respite. But if you turn back, I did not ask any reward
from you; my reward is only with Allah, and I am
commanded that I should be of those who submit (to Him).
But they rejected him; so We delivered him and those with
him in the ark, and We made them rulers and drowned
those who rejected Our Communications. Behold then,
what was the end of the people warned. (x. 71-73)

(5) Surely We sent Nuh to his people saying: Warn thy people
ere a painful chastisement overtake them.

He said: O my people! Surely I am a plain warner to you
bidding you to serve Allah and be mindful of your duty
to Him and obey me that He may forgive you your faults
and grant you respite for an appointed term. Surely the
term of Allah when it cometh cannot be deferred, if you
but know.

He said: O my Lord! Surely I have called my people night
and day but my calling only increaseth their aversion. And
whenever I call them to the true faith that Thou mayest
forgive them they thrust their fingers in their ears and
cover themselves with their garments and persist in their
infidelity, and proudly disdain my counsel. Moreover, I
invited them openly and spoke to them in public and
appealed to them in private and I said: Beg pardon of your
Lord, for He is ever Forgiving. He will cause the heavens
to pour down abundance of rain upon you and help you

with wealth and sons, and provide you gardens and make rivers flow for you. What aileth you that you hope not for benevolence from Allah, since He has crated you through various grades! Do you not see how Allah hath created the seven heavens one above another and hath placed the moon therein for a light and hath made the sun a lamp? And Allah hath made you grow out of the earth as a growth.

Then He will cause you to return to it, then will He bring you forth a new bringing forth. And Allah hath made the earth a wide expanse for you that you may go about therein through spacious paths.

Nuh said: My Lord! Verily they are disobedient to me and follow him whose wealth and children have added to him nothing but ruin. And they have devised a dangerous plot and they say to their own people: By no means forsake your gods, nor leave Wadd, nor Suwa', nor Yaghuth, and Ya'uq and Nasr. And indeed they have led astray many, and do Thou not increase and unjust in aught save error. Because of their evil deeds they were drowned and then made to enter fire and they did not find any helpers to protect them against Allah (lxxi. 1-25).

(6)　And certainly We formerly sent Nuh to his people. He said: I am a plain warner for you. You shall not serve any but Allah. Otherwise I fear for you the chastisement of a painful day. But the chiefs of those who disbelieved from among his people said: We do not consider thee but a mortal like ourselves and we do not see any follow thee except those who are the meanest of us by a rash judgement, neither do we see in thee any excellence over us; nay, we deem thee to be a liar.

He said: O my people! Tell me if I have not with me clear proof from my Lord and He has granted me mercy from Himself and it has been made obscure for you. Shall we compel you to receive it when you are averse to it? And O my people! I ask not wealth in return for what I preach. My reward is only with Allah and I am not going to drive away those who believe. Surely they shall meet their Lord and I perceive you are a people who are ignorant. And O my people! who will help me against Allah if I drive them away. Will you not therefore understand? And I do not say to you that I have the treasures of Allah in my power and neither do I say I know the unseen, nor do I say that I am an angel, nor do I say about those whom your eyes hold in mean estimation that Allah will never grant them any good--Allah knows best what is in their hearts--for then most surely I shall be of the unjust.

They said: O Nuh! Thou hast indeed disputed with us and lengthened the dispute with us. Now, therefore do thou bring on us what thou hast been threatening us with if thou art of the truthful ones.

He said: Allah alone shall bring it on you if He pleaseth and you will not escape it. And if I intend to give you good advice my advice will not profit you if Allah intendeth that He should cause you to perish. He is your Lord and to Him shall you be returned.

And it was revealed to Nuh: None of thy people shall believe except those who have already believed. Therefore do not grieve at what they do. And build the ark under Our eyes and according to Our instruction and do not speak to Me on behalf of the unjust. Surely they are deemed to be drowned (xi. 25-37)

III. Noah's Prayers

(7) And Nuh said: My Lord! Leave not upon the land any dweller from among the unbelievers. For, surely if Thou shouldst leave them they will lead astray Thy servants and will not beget any but immoral ungrateful offspring. My Lord! Forgive me and my parents and him who enters my house believing and the believing men and the believing women and do not increase the unjust in aught but destruction. (lxxi. 26-28)

(8) Before them the people of Nuh rejected the apostles. Yes! they denied Our servant and called him mad and reproached him. Therefore he called upon his Lord: My Lord! I am overpowered; come Thou then to my help (liv. 9-10)

IV. The Building of the Ark

(9) And he began to build the ark and whenever the chiefs among his people passed by him they derided him but he

said: Though you scoff at us now, we will scoff at you
hereafter even as you scoff at us. Then shall you know
who it is on whom will come a chastisement which will
disgrace him and on whom will lasting chastisement come
down. (Thus were they employed) until Our command
came and water gushed froth from the valley (Tannur)[3] and
We said to Nuh: Carry in it[4] two of all things, a pair, and
your own family--except those against whom the word has
already gone forth--and those who believe.[5] And there

---

3. There is generally a misunderstanding about the origin of the
Deluge due to a wrong interpretation of the word *Tannur* and *Fara* Lane's
Lexicon says that *fara* when used for water signifies gushing forth from
the earth and the word *Tannur* means not only an oven but also a reservoir
of water or place where the water of a valley collects. Hence the correct
translation will be that water gushed forth from the valley. Hence the
Deluge was the result of an exceptionally heavy rain and a severe cloud-
burst.

4. The words "all things of which pairs were to be taken" mean not
all animals existing on the earth, for the Deluge was only a local affair
that was brought about as a punishment upon the opponents of Noah.
By "all things" is apparently meant all things needed by Noah for the
sustenance of those in the ark. The same words occur in another place
in the Qur'an: "I found a woman ruling over them and she has been
granted of *all things*". (xxvii. 23)

Here too by "all things" is meant all things needed for here pomp
and glory.

But the Bible narrative makes Noah collect and lodge in his ark a
pair of each of the millions of species of animal, birds reptiles and of
everything that existed on the face of the earth. To collect and provide
not only accommodation for such a vast concourse of living things most
of which live upon one another and to provide food for them for not
less than a period of twelve months and ten days cannot be accepted
by any wild stretch of imagination to have been accomplished within the
ark, however, hugely built it might have been. A little reflection on the
description of this incident as given in Genesis, chapters 7 and 8, is enough
to show the absurdity of the whole story.

5. According to the Bible, only Noah and his family were saved, but
according to the Qur'an there were other people who believed in Noah
and they too were saved. There is thus this essential difference between
the two stories that all the righteous were saved along with Noah and
his family and all the wicked were destroyed including even two members
of Noah's family, namely, his son and his wife as given in the Qur'an
(see the verses that follow).

believed not with him but a few. And he said: Embark in it. In the name of Allah be its sailing and its anchoring: most surely my Lord is Forgiving, Merciful. (xi. 38-41)

V. The Deluge

(10) So We opened the gates of heavens with water pouring down and We caused the earth to gush forth its springs, so the water of heavens and earth gathered together according to measure already ordained. And We bore him on a vessel which was made of planks and nails, sailing before Our eyes, a reward for him who was denied and certainly We left it (the vessel) for a sign,[6] but is there anyone who will mind? (liv. 11-15).

VI. Noah's Son

(11) And it moved on with them amid waves like mountains and Nuh called out of his son who was separated from him: O my son! Embark with us and stay not with the unbelievers. He said: I will betake myself for refuge to a mountain[7] that shall protect me from water. Nuh said: There is no protection today from Allah's decree except for him on whom He shall have mercy.
And a wave intervened between them and so he became one of the drowned.[8]

---

6. There is no mention of the ark being left as a sign in the Bible but according to the Qur'an the ark was left as a sign for the coming generations. This is one of the astounding prophecies of the Qur'an, which was fulfilled when before the First Great War, a Russian air pilot Vilodemir Roskowisky discovered this ark on one of the mountain peaks of Armenia. This ark was lying buried under snow until 1822 C E. when an earthquake caused it to lie where it was discovered. A detailed account of this discovery is given in my article. "The Prophecies of the Qur'an" in the book *The Qur'an Speaks* under publication.

7. This shows that the Deluge came in a valley surrounded by mountains.

8. The Bible does not refer to the incident of the son of Noah being drowned along with the disbelievers. On the other hand it tells us that all his family was saved. It indeed speaks of a son of Noah but the difference is remarkable. It makes Noah first drunk to such an extent that

And it was said: O earth! Swallow up the waters and O
heavens! withhold thy rain. And the water was made to
abate and the decree was fulfilled and the ark rested on
Judi and it was said: Away with the unjust people.
And Nuh cried out to his Lord and said: My Lord' Surely
my son is of my family and Thy promise is surely true
and Thou art the most just of those who judge.
He said: O Nuh! Surely he is not of thy family; surely he
is of evil conduct; therefore ask not of Me that of which
thou hast no knowledge; surely I admonish thee lest thou
mayset be of the ignorant.
He said: My Lord! I seek refuge in Thee from asking Thee
that of which I have no knowledge and if Thou shouldst
not forgive me I shall be among the lost.
It was said: O Nuh! Come down from the ark with peace
from Us and blessings on thee and some nations that will
spring from those with thee and there shall be other
nations whom We will afford provision for a long time.
Then a painful doom from Us shall overtake them. These
are announcements relating to the unseen which We reveal
to thee (O Muhammad). Thou didst not know them,
neither thou nor thy people before thee. Therefore
persevere with patience. Surely the prosperous end is for
those who guard against evil. (xi 25-49)

The last verse of this passage is an answer to the lie fabricated
by the Christian critics of the Qur'an that the Bible is the source
of the stories of the prophets narrated in the Qur'an. It is indeed
a prophetical announcement refuting the anticipated libel that was
to be levelled against the Prophet by his prejudiced critics.

This verse also provides an answer to those misguided Muslims

---

he becomes naked: "And he drank of the wine, and was drunken; and
he was uncovered within his tent" (Genesis, 9: 21). One of his sons, Ham,
saw him in this condition and when Noah awoke from his wine he cursed
Canaan, the son of Ham, and condemned him to be "A servant of
servants", to his brethren. The story in all its details is entirely repugnant
to moral laws. Canaan suffers for the fault of his father. The Bible ascribes
the sin of getting drunk to a prophet of God. The story as narrated in
the Qur'an has a moral purpose behind it, but as related in the Bible
it skochs the very sense of morality.

who, under the spell of modernism, believe that the Qur'an makes use of the stories that were current among the Arabs of those days or among the people of the Book, only to draw some morals and that it is futile to seek any true historical background for them.

(12) And certainly We sent Nuh to his people and he said: O my people! Serve Allah. You have no other god besides God. Will you not then guard against evil? And the chiefs of those who disbelieved from among his people said: He is nothing but a mortal like yourselves who desires that he may have superiority over you and if Allah had pleased He could certainly have sent down angels. We have not heard of this among our fathers of yore. He is only a madman, so bear with him for a time.

He said: O my Lord! Help me against their calling me a liar. So, We revealed to him saying: Build the ark before our eyes and according to Our inspirations and when Our command is given and the valley overflows, take into it of everything a pair, two, and they followers except those among them against whom the word has gone forth and do not speak to Me on behalf of those who are unjust. Surely they shall be drowned. And when thou art firmly seated and those with thee in the ark, say: All praise is due to Allah Who delivered us from the unjust people and say: O my Lord! Cause me to alight a blessed alighting and Thou art the best to cause to alight. (xxiii. 23-29)

(13) And Nuh did certainly call upon Us and most excellent answerer to prayers are We. And We delivered him and his followers from the mighty distress. And We made his offspring the survivors and We perpetuated to him praise among the later generations. Peace on Nuh among the nations. Thus do We surely reward the doers of good. Surely he was of Our believing servants. Then We drowned the others. (xxxvii. 75-82)

VII. Noah's Age

Under the above verses we have covered almost all the important statements that refer to Noah and his people in the Qur'an. A very short notice of Noah contained in xxix. 14-15 adds that he remained among his people for 950 years. The Bible gives that to be the age of Noah, but there are indications that the reference here is to the abiding for 950 years of the Law preached by Noah, its place being then taken up by the Law of Abraham. According to the dates given in the Bible a period of 952 years elapsed between the advent of Noah and that of Abraham and the reference here may be of these 950 years.

In verses lxvi. 10 Noah's wife is mentioned along with Lot's wife and it is stated that both of them acted treacherously towards their righteous husbands and hence they were left to perish with the unbelievers. The Bible is silent in respect of these two women.

Now, before we see what moral lessons can be derived from the story of Noah, let our readers compare the account of Noah is given in the pages of the Qur'an which they have just now seen in the verses quoted above, with the one given in the Bible in the book of Genesis, chapters 6 to 9, and find out for themselves whether the Qur'an account of Noah could be based on the story given in the Bible: then they will see as clearly as the day the difference between a Divinely inspired account and a mere folklore.

VIII. Lessons from the Story of Noah and His People

(1) *Noah Ridiculed.* Appearances are generally deceptive and unreliable. When Noah was engaged in the construction of the ark on land at so great a distance from the sea-coast, his people who disbelieved in his mission used to ridicule him (xi. 38) at his seemingly foolish project. Here is a living example which demonstrates that the standard of knowledge based on mere sense perception is much lower than that of true knowledge which the prophets of God through Divine revelation have delivered to the world. Therefore one who puts his faith in Divine revelation and acts accordingly shall never be misled.

(2) *Insignificance of Blood Relationships in the Struggle for Truth.* The incident of Noah's son drowning before the eyes of his own father and Noah's helplessness to save him (xi. 45) is made an example to show that the basis of true kinship is not blood relationship but affinity of faith and moral outlook. Blood relatives may be counted as true relatives only if they are one with the believers in faith and righteousness, And if this common ground is wanting, a believer may have a superficial connection with such kinsmen but no hearty and sincere attachment can exist between

them. And in the conflict between evil and good if these kinsmen stand opposed to the believers, they shall have to be treated as strangers and on the same level with their disbelieving enemies. This was the touchstone on which the faithful were tested on the battle-fields of Badr and Uhud and history records that they stood the test and proved that in the struggle between truth and falsehood blood ties counted for nothing and their conduct was based on the verse "And those with him (the Prophet) are firm of heart against the unbelievers and compassionate among themselves." (xlviii. 29)

(3) *Ancestral Connections without True Faith and Action are no Guarantee for Salvation.* By citing the instance of Noah's son in the episode the Qur'an has forcefully pointed out how unbiased, impartial and conclusive is the verdict of God. The Meccan polytheists were under the impression that whatever they might do they would not invoke the displeasure of God as they were the descendants of Abraham and the favoured satellites of their gods and godnesses. The Jews and Christians also cherished similar notions. Even some of the misled Muslims are under the illusion that they shall inherit Paradise on the basis of their descent from the Prophet or their connection with some saintly person without exertion on their own part. Here is a spectacle of God's own apostle looking on his own son getting drowned before his very eyes and on the momentary impulse of paternal compassion supplicating to his God to save him, and is being rebuked and reproved for his misplaced affection. A father's prophethood was not able to save a depraved son. The law of recompense is at work for one and all and there is no exception to this rule.

(4) *The Good Only Shall Prosper Ultimately.* It is the law of nature that the good and the useful only survive. Noah and his followers though few in number and with no material resources at their disposal overcame their opponents in the long struggle between right and wrong. The Prophet Muhammad is here given the consolation that he will ultimately win as did the Prophet Noah. Here is a lesson for all sincere workers in the cause of truth not to be disheartened if they have to face hardships and disappointments on their way to conquer evil, for it is truth only that prospers in the end.

III

THE STORY OF THE PROPHETS
HUD AND SALIH
(May peace and blessings of God be upon them)

Hud and Salih were the prophets sent to the 'Ad and Thamud, two Arab tribes who were descended from their common ancestor Noah and his sons. The tribe of 'Ad traced their descent from 'Ad the grandson of Adam, who was the son of Sam, the son of Noah. They occupied a large tract of country in Southern Arabia extending from 'Umman at the month of the Persian Gulf to Hadramaut and Yemen at the southern end of the Red Sea. These people were tall in stature and were skilful builders. The long winding tracts of sand (*Ahqaf*) in their dominions were irrigated by canals.

The tomb of their Prophet Hud is still shown in Hadramaut about ninety miles from Mukalla. There are some rains and inscriptions in its neighbourhood. The Arabs go on pilgrimage to this tomb in the month of Rajab. These people are not mentioned in the Bible nor in their Prophet Hud.[9] But among the Arabs they were well known and references to these people are found in the poetry of the pre-Islamic era.

They were a powerful nation of their day and they were all idol-worshippers. They chiefly worshipped four deities named Saqi'ah, Hafizan, Raziqah and Salimah--the first, as they imagined,

---

9. The tribe of 'Ad with their Prophet Hud was so forgotten by history that it was actually in the risk of being dubbed legendary and fictitious by the "Wise men of the West" but for a miracle which has happened in our own time. Lt. Wellstead has discovered a Himyaritic inscription in Yemen province of Hadramount at a locality called Hish Ghorab. It has been deciphered and translated and a portion of it reads as follows:
"We are ruled by kings who were far from evil designs, chastisers of evil-doers, who ruled over us according to the laws of Prophet Hud...
For a full description see. Forester, *Historical Geography of Arabia.*

supplying them with rain, the second preserving them from all dangers abroad, the third providing them food for their sustenance, and the fourth, restoring them to health when affected with sickness.

The Prophet Hud was raised amidst them to bring them back to the worship of one God but very few believed in him. They were too proud of their achievements and thought themselves to be invincible. They committed acts of cruelty and violence and considered themselves safe in their fortresses and heeded not the warnings of their prophets. At last God's chastisement descended upon them and they were destroyed by a sand-storm blowing on them incessantly for eight days with a devastating effect, so much so that "it did not leave aught on which it blew but it made it like ashes". (li. 42).

Reference to these people and their Prophet Hud is found in the Qur'an in not less than fourteen places. Avoiding repetitions here are some quotations:

(1) And to the 'Ad We sent their brother Hud. He said: O my people! Serve Allah, you have no god other than Him. Will you not then keep away from evil and be mindful of your duty to Him. The chiefs of those who disbelieved from among his people said: Most surely we see thee in folly and indeed we think thee to be of the liars. He said: O my People! There is no folly in me but I am an apostle of the Lord of the worlds I convey to you the message of my Lord and I am a sincere adviser to you. Marvel ye that a reminder has come to you through a man from among you that He might warn you? Remember how He made you successors after Nuh's people and gave you growth of stature. Therefore remember the benefits of Allah that haply you may be successful.

They said: Hast thou come to us that we may serve Allah alone and give up what our fathers used to serve? Then bring upon us what thou threatens us with, if thou art of the truthful. He said: Indeed terror and wrath have already fallen upon you. Would you dispute with me over names which you and your fathers has given for which Allah hath sent no warrant. Wait then (for the consequences) I too with you will be of those who wait.

So, We delivered him and those with him by mercy from Us and We cut of the last of those who treated Our signs as lies and were not believers. (vii. 65-72)

(2) [Hud said:] O my people! I do not ask of you any recompense for this. My recompense is only with Him Who hath made me. Do you not then understand? O my people! Ask forgiveness of your Lord and turn to Him repenting. He will send on you clouds pouring down abundance of rain and add strength to your strength, only turn not back committing evil deeds.

They said: O Hud! Thou hast not brought to us any proof of thy mission and we are not going to abandon our gods on thy mere saying. We believe thee not. We cannot say aught but some of our gods have smitten thee with evil! He said: Surely I call Allah to witness and do you bear witness too, that I am clear of what you associate with Allah besides Him.

Therefore scheme against me all of you, and give me no respite, for, surely, I rely on Allah, my Lord and your Lord. No living creature there is but He holds it by its forelock. Right truly is the way in which my Lord dealeth. But if you turn away, still I have delivered to you the message with which I have been sent to you and my Lord will bring another people in your place and you cannot do Him any harm. Surely my Lord is the guardian over all things. And when Our decree came to pass, We saved Hud and those who believed with him by Our mercy and We delivered them from a harsh chastisement. (xi. 51-58)

(3) [Hud said]: Do you not build on every height a monument for vain delight, and do you not make strong fortresses that perhaps you may abide for ever? And when you lay hands on men, you lay hands like tyrants....He has given you abundance of cattle and children and gardens and fountains. Surely I fear for you the chastisement of a grievous day.

They said: It is the same to us whether thou admonish or are not of the admonishers. This is naught but a custom of the ancients and we are not they who shall be chastised. So they denied him and therefore We destroyed them.

Most surely there is a sign in this, yet most of them do not believe and most sure thy Lord is the Mighty, the Merciful (xxvi. 128-140).

(4) As to the 'Ad, they were unjustly proud in the land and they said: Who is mightier in strength than we? Could they not see that Allah who created them is Mightier than they in strength and yet they denied Our revelations. So, We sent on them a furious blast in unlucky days that We may make them taste the chastisement of abasement in this world's life and certainly the chastisement of the hereafter is much more abasing, and they shall not be protected. (xli. 15-16)

(5) When they saw it as a closed appearing in the sky advancing towards their valley, they said: This is a cloud which will give us rain. Nay, it is what you sought to hasten on, a blast of wind in which is a painful chastisement, destroying everything by the command of its Lord, and morning found them so that naught could be seen except their empty dwellings. Thus repay We a wicked people. (xlvi. 24-25)

(6) The 'Ad treated the truth as a lie, so how great was My chastisement after My warnings! Surely We sent on them an intensely cold wind in a day of bitter ill-luck, tearing men away as if they were the trunks of palm-trees torn up from their roots. (liv. 18-20)

(7) As to the 'Ad, they were destroyed by a roaring violent blast which He made to prevail against them for seven nights and eight days unintermittingly, so that thou mightest have seen the people therein prostrate as if they were hollow trunks of palm-tree. (lxix. 6-7)

In one of the above passage God Himself points out that the fate of the 'As should be taken as a sign by those who disbelieve in His revelations. This is addressed to the opponents of the Prophet Muhammad warning them of a similar fate and consoling the believers that they will soon be delivered of the persecutions they were undergoing in the way of truth.

These quotations show that whenever a prophet was raised among any people, the people got divided into two groups. On one side was the prophet with his little band of followers, who believed in his mission and underwent hardships as a test of their faith, and on the other side the whole community, arrogantly defying the prophet and persecuting him and his followers. The Prophet Muhammad and his followers found themselves in a parallel situation at Mecca. In the stories of the prophets gone by a warning is given to those who were opposing them, of their coming fate, if they refused to head the good counsel which was being given them. This has indeed been the Law of God that those who pursued the way of truth with steadfastness and patience ultimately prevailed over their enemies. It is a lesson to be born in mind by all those persons as well as communities who exert themselves in the way of God to establish truth and justice that triumph shall be finally theirs.

The Thamud and Their Prophet Salih. The tribe called Thamud, otherwise known as the second 'Ad, is often mentioned in the Qur'an conjointly with the first 'Ad. This tribe flourished more than two hundred years after 'Ad. They occupied the territory known as al-Hajr and the plain known as Wadi al-Qura which forms the southern boundary of Syria and the northern one of Arabia. The cut the rocks to make dwelling places and after having carved them took up their abode therein.[10]

These rock-habitations are up to this very day known by the name of *Asalib.* Almost every Arab as well as several foreigners who have travelled in Arabia can bear testimony to the existence

---

10. R.A. Nicholson who has compiled a literary history of the Arabs states:

"In north Arabia, between Hadjaz and Syria dwelt a kindred race of Thamudites described in the Qur'an (vii. 27) as inhabiting houses which they cut for themselves in the rocks. Evidently Muhammad did not know the true nature of the hewn chambers which are still to be seen at Hijr (Middian Saleh) a week's journey northward from Medina and which are proved by Nabathean inscription engraved on them to have been sepulchral monuments."

But Nicholson is woefully wrong in his surmises Dr. Chrichton the author of a *History of Arabia,* has mentioned buildings and dwelling places excavated at Kerak, the ancient Petra, which have been cut in rocks. One of these localities goes by the name of "The Treasury of Pharaoh" and an illustration of this is found in the book. This is one of the several instances which establish the super-human knowledge of the Qur'an and its exponent the Prophet.

of these rock-habitations which stand there at once to satisfy curiosity and to afford information respecting the nations which made them. These habitations likewise corroborate and bear testimony to the truth to that portion of the history of the Thamud tribe which is mentioned in the Holy Qur'an, but strangely enough not a trace of it is found in the literature of the Israelites.

The Prophet on his expedition to Tabuk passed through this tract of land called al-Hajr and he gave a sermon on these archaeological remains to his followers which is recorded in the traditions. We have in India similar habitations excavated for religious purposes in the mountains known by the name of Ellora and Ajanta which demonstrate the skill and engineering talent of the ancients.

Salih their prophet was a descendant in the sixth generation after Thamud, the great ancestor of the tribe after whom it is known. He tried hard to prevent his people from idol-worship but only a few believed in him and the rest were destroyed by a volcanic eruption which rained stones upon them. Their story is told in the Qur'an in the following verses:

(8) And to the Thamud We sent their brother Salih. He said: O my people! Serve Allah. You have no God other than Him. Clear proof indeed has come to you from your Lord. This is as Allah's she-camel[11] for you, a sign. Therefore

---

11. A she-camel was fixed as a sign and they were warned that if they slew her punishment would overtake them. Neither the Qur'an nor any reliable saying of the Holy Prophet lends any support to the numerous legends--the miraculous appearance and prodigious size of the she-camel and their slaying of it was a sign that they would neither accept the truth nor cease persecuting Salih and his followers.

It may be noted here that there is nothing strange that a she-camel should be given as a sign when even how we can see that a roughly constructed house known as the Ka'bah is given as a sign to the whole world, so that whoever tries to destroy it perishes himself. The ordinary house built by rough stones is a much greater sign than Salih's living she-camel.

It appears that the springs of water were few, and access to these was probably guarded so that they were open only at particular times. Salih must have demanded that the she camel should also be given a drink along with others and that she should be allowed to pasture on the land without any hindrance. As we find in quotation No. 11 they leave her alone to pasture on Allah's earth and do not do her any harm. Otherwise painful chastisement will overtake you. And remember, when He made you successors after 'Ad and settled you in the land--you make mansions on its plain and hew out houses in the mountains--remember therefore Allah's benefits and do not act corruptly in the land making mischief.

The chiefs of those who behaved proudly among his people said to those who were considered weak, to those who believed from among them: Are you sure that Salih is sent by his Lord? They said: Surely, we are believers in what he has been sent with. Those who were haughty said: Surely we deny of what you believe in. So, they slew the she-camel and revolted against their Lord's commandments and they said: O Salih! Bring us what thou threatenest us with if thou art one of the apostles.

Then the earthquake overtook them, so they became motionless bodies in their abodes. Then he (Salih) turned away from them and said: O my people! I did certainly deliver to you the message of my Lord and I gave you good counsel but you did not love those who give good advice. (vii. 73-79)

The punishment which overtook the Thamud is described under different names. In the above passage it is called earthquake. In another place it is called a rumbling noise which precedes an earthquake.

(9) They said: O Salih! Surely thou were one amongst us in whom great expectations were placed before this. Dost thou now forbid us from worshipping what our fathers worshipped? And as to that which thou callest us to, most surely we are in disquieting doubt.

He said: O my people! Tell me if I have clear proof from my Lord and He has granted to me mercy from Himself. Who will then help me against Allah if I disobey Him?

---

had laid a plan for the murder of their prophet and the slaying of the she-camel was a sign that they were about to execute their final plan against Salih himself but before they could do so, God's punishment overtook them and they were destroyed one and all except a few who believed in Salihi.

Therefore you would add to me naught save predition. O my people! This will be as Allah's she-camel for you a sign. Therefore leave her to pasture on Allah's earth and do not touch her with evil, for, then, a near chastisement will overtake you.

But they slew her; so, he said: Enjoy yourselves in your abodes for three days, that is a threat not to be belied. So, when Our decree came to pass, We saved Salih and those who believed with him, by mercy from Us from the disgrace of that day. Surely your Lord is the Strong, the Mighty. And the rumbling overtook those who were unjust; so they became motionless bodies in their abodes as though they had never dwelt in them. (xi. 62-68)

(10) The Thamud denied the apostles. When their brother Salih said to them: Will you not abstain from evil and fear the Lord and do good: Surely I am a faithful apostle to you. Therefore guard yourselves against the punishment of Allah and obey me. I do not ask of you any compensation for it. My compensation is with the Lord of the worlds. Will you be left secure in what is hete, in gardens and fountains, and corn-fields and palm-trees having fine fruits layer upon layer.

And you hew houses out of the mountains exultingly. Therefore guard against the punishment of Allah and obey me, and do not obey the binding of the extravagant who make mischief in the land and do not act aright.

They said: Thou art only of the deluded ones. Thou art naught but a mortal like ourselves, so, bring a sign if thou are one of the truthful. He said: This is a she-camel. She shall have her portion of water, and you your portion of water on an appointed time. And do not touch her with evil, lest the chastisement of a grievous day should overtake you.

But they stabbed her and then regretted on the morrow when the chastisement overtook them. Most surely there is a sign in this, but most of them do not believe. And most surely thy Lord is the Mighty, the Merciful. (xxvi. 141-159)

(11) And certainly We sent to the Thamud their brother Salih

(who said): Serve Allah, and lo! they become two parties
contending with each other. He said: O my people! Why
do you seek to hasten on the evil before the good? Why
do you not ask forgiveness of Allah so that you may be
dealt with mercifully. They said: We have met with ill-
luck on account of thee and on account of those with thee.
He said: The ills of which you augur depends on Allah
and you are a people on trial.

And there were in the city nine persons who committed
excesses in the land and did not act aright. They said:
Swear to each other by Allah that we will certainly make
a sudden attack on him and his family by night, then we
will say to his heir: We did not witness the destruction
of his family and verily we speak the truth.[12]

And they planned a plan and We planned a plan and they
perceived it not. See then what was the end of their plan.
We destroyed them and their people, all of them, and for
their iniquities their homes have become empty ruins.
Most surely there is a sign in this for a people who
understand. And We delivered those who believed and
who guarded themselves against evil. (xxvii. 45-53)

(12) The Thamud rejected the warning and so they said: What!
A single mortal from among us! Shall we follow him? Most

---

12. Here is a parallel circumstances in the life of the Holy Prophet.
Among his persecutors there were nine very influential members of the
Quraish, eight of whom were slain at Badr the exception being Abu Lahab
who died at Mecca on hearing the news of the defeat at Badr. Their names
were (i) Abu Jahal, Mut'im bin 'Adiyy, (iii) Shaiba bin Rabi'ah, (iv) 'Utbah
bin Rabi'ah, (v) Walid bin 'Utbah, (vi) Umayyah bin Khalaf, (vii) Nadar
bin al-Harth, (viii) 'Aqabah bin Mu'ait and (ix) Abu Lahab.
There seems to be a prophetical reference here to the plot against
the Holy Prophet, for the same plan was agreed upon by the Quraish
to do away with him. It should be borne in mind that the revelation of
these verses bleongs to an early period. The plot against the prophet's
life was to have been executed in the following manner: One man from
every tribe of the Quraish was selected to make a squad who should take
the Prophet unawares. They were to thrust their swords into his body
simultaneously, so that no particular tribe could be held guilty. This was
agreed upon immediately, before the Prophet's flight to Medina and thus
the incident relating to Salih is meant as prophecy.

surely we shall in that case be in sure error and distress. Has the reminder been made to light upon him from among us? Nay, he is an insolent liar.

Tomorrow shall they know who the liar is, the insolent one. Surely We are going to send a she-camel as a trial for them. Therefore do thou, O Salih, watch them and be patient and inform them that the water should be shared between them and every drinking shall be witnessed. But they called their companion who took the sword and slew her. How great was them My chastisement after My warnings. Surely we sent upon them a single cry and they became like the dry twigs which the builder of a cattle-fold collects. (liv. 23-31)

In the stories of these two Prophets Hud and Salih, a prophetic announcement is made to the Quraish, the opponents of the Prophet that their fate would be no better if they did not cease to commit atrocities on the Prophet and his little band of faithful followers.

IV

THE STORY OF THE PROPHET
IBRAHIM (ABRAHAM)

(May peace and the blessings of God be on him)

The story of Abraham is very widely scattered in the pages of the Qur'an and he is spoken of for more than forty times. This due to the fact that he was accepted by all the communities that resided in Arabia during the time of the Prophet, namely, the Jews, the Christians, and the idolatrous Arabs, every one of when claimed him as their ancestory, though none of them practised his religion. It is for this reasons that they are again and again invited to the religion of Abraham, the upright one. The Qur'an speaks of his noble character in the following verses:

I. Abraham's Character

(1) Surely Ibrahim was an exemplar, obedient to Allah, by nature upright, and he was not of the polytheists. He was grateful for Our bounties; We chose him and guided him unto a right path, and We gave him good in this world, and in the next he will most surely be among the righteous. (xvi. 120-121)

(2) Ibrahim the upright one, and Allah chose him as friend. (iv. 125)

(3) And mention Ibrahim in the Book. Surely he was a truthful man and a prophet.[13] (xix. 41)

---

13. Against this testimony of the Qur'an the Bible records the following about him: "And it came to pass, when he was come near to enter into Egypt, that he said unto Sara his wife. Behold now, I know that thou art a fair woman to look upon: Therefore it shall come to pass, when the Egyptians see thee, that they shall say, This is his wife: and they will kill me, but they will save thee alive. Say, I pray thee, thou

(4) And Ibrahim came to his Lord with a free heart. (xxxvii. 84)

(5) Most surely Ibrahim was forbearing, tender-hearted and oft-returning to Allah. (xi. 75)

(6) And We perpetuated praise to him (Ibrahim) among the later generations. Peace be on Ibrahim. Thus do We reward the doers of good. Surely he was one of our believing servants-and We showered Our blessings on him. (xxxvii. 108-113)

(7) We made him (Ibrahim) pure in this world and in the hereafter; he is most surely among the righteous. When his Lord said to him, Submit, he said: I submit myself to the Lord of the worlds. (ii. 130-131)

(8) Ibrahim was not a Jew nor a Christian but he was Hanif (i.e., firm in sticking to a right state) and a Muslim (i.e., resigned to God) and he was not one of the polytheists. (iii. 66).

(9) And who has a better religion than he who submits himself entirely to Allah? And he is the doer of good to others and follows the faith of Ibrahim and Hanif. (iv. 152).

---

art my sister, that it may be well with me for thy sake, and my soul shall live because of these. And it came to pass, that when Abraham was come into Egypt, the Egyptians be held the woman that she was very fair. The princes also of Pharaoh saw her and commended her before Pharaoh: and the woman was taken into Pharaoh's house. And he entreated Abraham well for her sake: and he had sheep, and oxen, and the asses, and menser ants and midservants, and she-asses and cames. And the Lord plagued Pharaoh and his house with great plagues because of Sara: Abraham's wife And Pharaoh called Abraham, and said, What is this that thou hast done unto me? Why didst thou not tell me that she was thy wife? Why saidst thou, She is my sister? So I might have taken her to me to wife; now therefore behold thy wife, take her, and go thy way." (Gen. 12: 11-19)

Again in Genesis 20: 2-13 the Bible makes Abrahim utter a similar lie to Abemelech, king of Gerar, to save himself from an imminent danger. What a contrast between the teachings of the Qur'an and those of the books of the Jews and the Christians and yet they have the cheek to assert that the Prophet got his inspiration from the stories of the Bible!

II. Abraham's Leniency Towards His Enemies

Another trait of Abraham's character was that he was very lenient towards his foes, so much so that he pleaded for Lut's people to be saved though he knew that they were transgressors.

(10) He began to plead with Us for Lut's people; most surely Ibrahim was forbearing, tender-hearted and oft-returning to Allah. (xi. 75-79)

(11) My Lord: Surely they (the idols) have led many men astray. Then, whoever follows me, he is surely of me, and whoever disobeys me, Thou surely art Forgiving, Merciful. (xiv. 36)

He thus invoked Divine mercy even for his enemies and this notwithstanding that he had to sever his connections with them.

III. Abraham's Preachings[14]

Abraham was a strong preacher against idol-worship and polytheism of every kind and he broke the idols after openly giving his people a warning of what he intended to do. This constituted a prophecy that idols which polluted the Ka'bah during the Prophet's time would ultimately be broken which actually got fulfilled on his taking over Mecca.

(12) And Ibrahim said to his father Adhar,[15] Taketh thou idols for gods? Surely I see thee and the people in manifest error;--And when the night grew dark upon him he beheld a star: said he: Is this my Lord? So when it set, he said: I love not the setting ones. Then when he saw the moon rising, he said: Is this my Lord?

---

14. There is no mention of Abraham's preachings in the Bible. Only in one place (Gen. 20: 7) he is mentioned as a prophet and even here nothing is said about his prophetic mission and why he had to migrate from his native land to other places. But the Qur'an points out that when his people tried to cast him into fire and God delivered him from it he had to flee from his native land and take refuge in Palestine.

15. The Bible gives his father's name as Tarah and in the Talmud it is given as Terah but Eusibius the Great historian calls him Athar which corresponds to the Arabic name Adhar. Was Muhammad acquainted with the works of the Greek historian is a point for the Christian critics to prove.

So when it set he said: If my Lord hath not guided me I should certainly have been of the erring ones. Then, when he saw the sun rising, he said: Is this my Lord? Is this the greatest? So when it also set he said: O my people! Surely I am clear of what you set up with Allah. Surely I have turned myself wholly to Him as one by nature upright who originated the heavens and the earth and I am not of polytheists.[16]

And his people disputed with him. He said: Do you dispute with me respecting Allah when He has guided me indeed? And I do not fear those that you set up with Him unless my Lord pleases. My Lord comprehends all things is His knowledge. Will you not then mind? And how should I fear what you have set up with Him while you do not fear for what you have set up with Allah for which He has not sent down to you any warranty. Which then of the two parties is surer of security? Answer me that if you know. Those who believe and do not mix up their faith with any semblance of polytheistic attitude, those are they who shall be secure and those are they who are guided aright. (vi. 75-83)

(13) And mention Ibrahim in the book. Surely he was truthful man and a prophet. He said to his father: O my sire! Why dost thou worship what neither hears nor sees nor does it avail thee in the least? O my sire! The knowledge has come to me which has not come to thee; therefore follow me and I will guide thee unto the right path. O my sire! Serve not the devil, surely the devil is disobedient to the Beneficent God. O my Sire! Surely I fear lest a punishment from the Beneficent God overtake thee, then thou shalt be a friend of the devil.

---

16. The people of Abraham were not only idolaters but also worshippers of the heavenly bodies. These words are uttered by way of surprise referring to his people's beliefs to make them realise their error by showing that what they call a god disappears at times and therefore does not deserve to be worshipped. These words do not contain Abraham's conviction as he was a staunch believer in the unity of God.

He said: Dost thou reject my gods, O Ibrahim? If thou dost
not desist, I will certainly revile thee. It is better that thou
leave me for a time. He said: Peace be on thee. I will pray
to my Lord to forgive thee. Surely He is ever Gracious to
me and I will withdraw from thee and what thou callest
on besides. Allah, and I will call upon My Lord: Maybe
I shall not remain unblessed in calling upon my Lord. (xix,
41-48)

(14) Have you not considered him[17] who disputed with Ibrahim
about his Lord, because Allah had given him the kingdom?
When Ibrahim said: My Lord is He Who giveth life and
causeth death, he answered: I also give life and cause
death, Then Ibrahim said: Surely Allah causeth the sun
to rise from the east, then do thou make it rise from the
west. Thus he who disbelieved was confounded and Allah
doth not guide the unjust people. (ii. 258).

(15) And certainly We gave to Ibrahim his rectitude before, and
We knew him fully well. When he said to his sire and
his people: What are these images to whose worship you
cleave, they said We found our fathers worshipping them.
He said: Certainly you have been both you and your fathers
in manifest error. They said: Hast thou brought to us the
truth or art thou one of the trifilers: He said: Nay, your
Lord is the Lord of the heavens and the earth Who brought
them into existence and I am of those who bear witness
to this. And by Allah I will certainly strive against you
idols after you have gone away and turned your backs.
Then he broke them into pieces except the chief of them
that haply they may return to him. They said: Who has
done this to our gods? Most surely he is one of the evil-
doers. They said: We heard a youth called Ibrahim make
mention of them Said they: Then bring him before the eyes
of the people that they may testify. They said: Hast thou
done this to our gods, O Ibrahim? He said: Whosoever

---

17. This personal pronoun is taken as referring to Nimrud, the King
of Ur in Chaldea, the home town of Abraham. There is no mention of
this incident in the Bible.

has done it has done it; the chief of them is this, therefore ask them if they can speak.[18] Then they turned to themselves and said: Surely you yourselves are the unjust. Then they were made to hang down their heads. And they said: Certainly thou knowest that they do not speak. He said: When! Do you then serve besides. Allah what brings you not any benefit at all nor does it harm you? Fie on you and on what you serve beside Allah! What! Do you not then understand? They said: Burn him and stand by your gods if you are going to do anything. We said: O Fire! Be coolness and peace for Ibrahim. And they sought to lay a plot against him but We made them the greatest losers. And we rescued him and Lut and brought them to the land which We had blessed for all people. (xxi. 51-71)

(16) And We sent Ibrahim when he said to his people: Serve Allah and be careful of your duty to Him. This is best for you if you did but know. You only worship idols besides Allah and you invent a lie. Surely, they whom you serve besides Allah do not control for you any sustenance; therefore seek the sustenance from Allah and serve Him and be grateful to Him, for to Him you shall be brought back. And if you reject the truth, nations before you did indeed reject the truth and nothing is incumbent on the apostle but a plain delivery of the message;...So nought was the answer of his people except that they said: Slay him or burn him. Then Allah delivered him from the fire. Most surely there are signs in this for a people who believe. (xxix. 16-18, 24)

---

18. The incident of the breaking of the idols is also not mentioned in the Bible, but it is described in Midrash Rabah in which it is alleged that Abraham told a lie by saying that the chief idol broke the other idols. In the version given in the Qur'an Abraham does not absolve himself from the act but says: "Whosoever has does it has done it: the chief of them is this, therefore ask them if they can speak," This was to give them a convincing proof of the futility of their devotion to such things which were not capable of protecting themselves Even this little incident shows that the source of this is not the Jewish traditions.

(17) When he (Ibrahim) said to his sire and his people: What is it that you worship but a lie--gods besides Allah do you desire? What is then you opinion about the Lord of the worlds. Then he looked at the stars looking up once, then he said: Surely I am sick of your worshipping these. And they turned away their backs and went away from him. Then turned he to their gods and said: Will you not eat? what is the matter with you that you do not speak? Then he attacked them smiting them with the right hand. Then his people came towards him hastening. Said he: What! Do you worship what you hew out? And Allah has created you and has created that which you make. They said: Build for him a structure and then cast him into the burning fire. And they sought to lay a plot against him but We brought them low. (xxxvii. 85-90)[19]

IV. Announcement of the Birth of Ishmael and the Vision of Abraham

After migrating from his native country Chaldea Abraham had to wander about into Syria, Palestine and Egypt preaching against idol-worship, so much so that he became quite aged and, as the Bible record shows, he was eighty-six years old when Ishmael was born to him from Hagar (Genesis 16:16) The Qur'an does not indulge itself in unnecessary details which have no bearing on the life of the Prophet Muhammad for whom these stories are narrated. It touches upon those features of the story in a prophetical style which correspond to similar features of the life of the Prophet and his mission and therefore we do not find in the Qur'an how he took Hagar to wife and how she was left with the infant child in the wilderness of Batha where now the Ka'bah stands and how the spring of Zamzam emerged from beneath the foot of the infant Ismael. A passing reference is made in ii. 159 of the two hillocks

---

19. This incident is also not mentioned in the Bible but in Gen., 15: 7 its reference is given in these words; "I am the Lord that brought thee out of the Ur of the Chaldnees". But the word Ur is translated by the Jews and the Eastern Christians as fire (*vide*, Hyde, *Religion of the Persians*, p. 73) and in the Syrian calendar 25 January is set apart for the commemoration of the Delivery of Abraham from fire of the Chaldees.

called Safa and Marwah, the scene of Hagar's running to and fro in quest of water for her thirsting child and which are now become part of the rites of pilgrimage in commemoration of the resignation of Hagar to the will of God.

But the Qur'an gives in vivid words Abraham's character in which he represents the Prophet in his entire submission to God, so much so that when he receives a commandment in his vision to sacrifice his only son Ismael, he does not hesitate to do it. This no doubt contained a prophetic reference to the complete submission of the Prophet and his followers who were asked to say:

(18) My prayer and my sacrifices, my life and my death are all for Allah, the Lord of the worlds. (vi. 163)

and who showed their willingness to lay down their own lives and the lives of those dearest to them to defend the truth. And now read what the Qur'an says:

(19) We gave him the good news of a boy possessing forbearance and when he attained to working age with him he said: O my son! Surely I have seen in a vision that I should sacrifice thee.[20] Tell me then what thy opinion is.

---

20. It may be remarked here that the Qur'an speaks of Ishmael as the son whom Abraham was ordered to sacrifice as it speaks of the good news of Isaac's birth being given to Ibrahim after the incident of the sacrifice, (xxxvii. 112). This contradicts the Bible's statement which speaks of Isaac as being the son who was ordered to be sacrificed. But according to the account given in the Bible there is a clear self-contradiction which can be seen from the following:

(i) When Ishmael was born Abraham was eighty-six years old (see Genesis, 16:6) but when Isaac was born his age was 100 years (see Genesis, 21:5). As such Isaac cannot be called "Thy only son" in verses 2, 12, and 16 of Genesis, 22; Ishmael was then fourteen years senior to Isaac and in his presence Isaac cannot be called "Thy only son". This title should go to Ishmael alone. Therefore it is quite evident that the text has been altered in favour of Issac.

(ii) When the command for circumcision was given Ishmael was thirteen years old (see Genesis, 17:25) and when Isaac was born he was circumcised when only eight days old (Genesis 21:4). In this chapter it is stated that Hager was sent away into the wilderness of Beer Sheba with her son on the instigation of Sarah out of mere jealousy which does

He said: O my father! Do what thou art commanded; if
Allah please, thou wilt find me of the patient ones.
So, when they both submitted and he threw him down
upon his forehead, We called out of him: O Ibrahim! Thou
hast indeed shown the truth of the vision. Surely thou do
We reward the doers of good...And We gave him the good
news of Ishaq a prophet among the good ones, and We
showered Our blessings on him and on Ishaq; and of their
offspring are the doers of good and also those who are
clearly unjust to their own selves. (xxxvii. 10-113)

V. The Birth of Issac

As we have pointed out above, the Qur'an mentions the birth
of Issac as a good news to Abraham when he proved his unstinted*
submission to God's commandment by trying to sacrifice his only
son Ishmael in fulfilment of his vision. This is described in the
Qur'an in following verses:

(20) And certainly Our messengers came to Ibrahim with good
news. They said: Peace, Peace, said he, and he made no
delay in bringing a roasted calf, but when he saw that their

---

little credit to a prophet's wife. This again is evidence enough that Isaac
could never be called "Thy only son"

(*iii*) After the incident of sacrifice was over it is stated that Abraham
went and lived at Beer Sheba where Hagar was left (see Genesis 22: 19)
which is again evidence enough that Ishmael was taken to be sacrificed
and when he was rescued by the substitution of a ram, naturally Abraham
took his son back to his mother.

(*iv*) There is again a contradiction in the Bible where it states that
both Hagar and Ishmael dwelt in the wilderness of Paran (Genesis, 21:
21) because it was not Paran but Beer Sheba where she was left with
the lad as stated in Genesis, 21: 14. The Bible commentators have laboured
in vain to locate Paran in Beer Sheba which is the name of a mountain
in the valley of Mecca. So all these statements of the Bible go to prove
beyond doubt that it was Ishmael who was ordered to be sacrificed and
not Isaac.

(*v*) Moreover both the Bible and the Qur'an agree that a ram was
substituted in place of the lad, but the sacrifice of a lamb is commemorated
among the descendants of Ishmael, the Arabs, and not among Isaac's
which is an additional testimony to the truth of what the Qur'an says.

hands did not extend towards it[21] he deemed them strange and conceived fear of them.

They said: Fear not, surely we are sent to Lut's people. And his wife who was standing by laughed when We gave her the good news of the birth of Ishaq and after Ishaq (of a son) Ya'qub. She said: O wonder! How shall I bear a son when I am an extremely old woman and this my husband an extremely old man? Most surely this is a strange thing. They said: Wonderest thou at Allah's bidding? The mercy of Allah and His blessings be on you, O people of the house! Surely He is praiseworthy and Glorious. (xi, 69-73)

VI. Abraham's Connection with the Ka'bah

According to the Qur'an, Abraham left Ishmael and his mother Hagar in the valley of Batha (Mecca) and not in the wilderness of Beer Sheba stated in the Bible, for Paran is not in Beer Sheba. This is evident from the prayer of Abraham which is given in the Qur'an in the following words:

(21) O our Lord? I have settled a part of my offspring in a valley unproductive of fruit near Thy sacred House, our Lord, that they may keep up prayer. (xiv. 37)

From this it is clear that Abraham had left Ishmael in Arabia in accordance with a Divine commandment and not at the instigation of his wife Sarah as that would have been an injustice done to Hagar and her child and such a course of action would have become a stigma on the character of a prophet of God. In fact it was all done in accordance with a Divine scheme, so that the stone which the builders rejected should become the head of the corner (Matthew, 21: 42, and Ps., 118: 22). Ishmael was that stone, for, whereas from the descendants of Israel came numerous prophets, from the descendants of him who was cast into the wilderness and whom the Israelites began to hate, though he was

---

21. This contradicts the Bible's statement (Gen., 18:18) which says that they ate the roasted calf and other food provided by Abraham, but the contrary was mentioned by the Rabbins (see Rodwell's not on page 221 of his translation of the Qur'an) which shows that the Qur'an has spoken the truth.

their brother, came the last to the prophets who became the head
of the corner.

And now the building of the Ka'bah is stated in the following
verses:

(22) And when We assigned to Ibrahim the site of the House,
(saying) do not associate with Me aught and purify My
House for those who make the circuit and stand to pray
and bow and prostrate themselves; and proclaim among
men the pilgrimage. (xxii. 26-27)

(23) And when Ibrahim and Isma'il were raising the foundations of the House (they prayed): Our Lord! Accept from
us; surely Thou art the Hearing, the Knowing. Our Lord!
And make us both submissive to Thee and raise from our
offspring a nation submitting to Thee and show us our
ways of devotion and turn to us mercifully. Surely Thou
art the Oft-Returning to mercy, the Merciful.

And O Lord! raise up in their midst an apostle from among
them who shall recite to them Thy revelations and teach
them the Law and wisdom and purify them. Surely Thou
art the Mighty, the Wise. (ii. 127-129)

(24) We made the House a resort for men and a place of security
(Saying) : Take as your place of worship the place where
Ibrahim stood to pray. And We enjoined Ibrahim and
Islam'il (saying): Purify My House for those who visit it
and those who meditate therein and those who bow down
and those who prostrate themselves.

And call to mind the occasion when Ibrahim prayed: My
Lord! Make this a town of security and provide its people
who fruits, such of them as believe in Allah and the last
day. (ii. 125-126)

(25) And call to mind the occasion when Ibrahim said: My Lord!
Make this city secure and save me and my children from
worshipping idols--and make the hearts of people yearn
towards them and provide them with fruits, that haply
they may be grateful. (xiv. 35-37)

We have given already a fuller amount of Abraham and Ishmael
and their connection with the pilgrimage of Mecca in the chapter
entitled "Hajj" of the second book of this series called *Islam in
Practical Life* and, therefore, the account given in the above-quoted
verses is enough to show that the name of Abraham and Ishmael
have remained connected with the sanctuary at Mecca where a spot

called "the standing place of Ibrahim" existed from ancient times.

LESSONS FROM THE STORY OF ABRAHAM
I. The Ordeal of Fire

When Abraham broke the idols and left their chief idol unhurt to demonstrate that the idols had no power either to cause harm to or bestow benefit upon any person, and they were as helpless as mere stones of which they were made, and, therefore, it was against the dignity of a human being to pay homage to them which was rightly due to God alone, his people, instead of appreciating his argument against the helplessness of their deities, got wild with him, and as a penalty for committing that sacrilege, cast him into the fire. But Abraham was a man of staunch faith in God and he knew that nothing could cause him harm against the will of God. He came out of that ordeal unscathed to the utter discomfiture of his opponents, and the pronouncement of God, "O Fire! Be thou a comfort and security for Ibrahim." gave the faithful a lesson that those who resign themselves entirely to God shall have no fear nor shall they grieve.

II. The Ordeal of Sacrifice

The Qur'an says: "By no means shall you attain to righteousness unless you spend away in the way of God the things that you love most." (iii. 91)

Abraham's second biggest ordeal was the order to sacrifice his only son Ishmael, the prop of his old age, to demonstrate that his love of God superseded all wordly considerations. When this order was given he was in his nineties and there was no hope of having any other child after Ishmael. But those whose hearts are satiated with the love of God find no room for any other passion in their hearts. Abraham again stood the test and "When he threw him (his son) down upon his forehead We called out to him: 'O Ibrahim! Thou hast indeed shown the truth of thy vision.'" (xxxvii. 103-105)

What was the meed that Abraham got for his superb sacrifice for the sake of God? The Qur'an tells us that God made him the ancestor of three great nations of the world, the Jews, the Christians, and the Muslims, and kept his name alive as a symbol of righteousness and unflinching resolution in the way of God.

(26) And when his Lord tried Abraham with certain commands

> and he carried them out, He said: I will make thee a leader
> of men. (ii. 134)

And the Prophet, by introducing the rite of sacrifice in the 'Id-
ul-Adha among his followers, perpetuated the commemoration of
the sacrifice of Abraham till the Day of Resurrection and fulfilled
the prophecy of the Bible wherein it was said:

> I will make of thee a great nation, and I will bless thee,
> and make thy name great; and thou shalt be blessing: and
> I will bless them that bless thee, and curse him that curseth
> thee: and in thee shall all families of the earth be blessed.
> (Genesis 21: 2-3)

by introducing the *Durud* or blessing on Abraham in the Muslim
prayers which is recited daily several times by tens of millions of
Muslims all over the world invoking the blessing of God on
Abraham and his progeny.

Here is a lesson for every Muslim to remember that God never
suffers the good deeds of the believers to go waste. The Qur'an
gives us the assurance that:

> (27) Allah wasteth not the reward of the believers. (iii. 170)
>
> (28) Surely We do not waste the reward of the righteous. (vii.
>   170)
>
> (29) Allah does not waste the reward of the doers of good. (ix.
>   120)
>
> (30) This is the promise of Allah and Allah fails not in His
>   promise. (ix. 20)

Every Muslim should therefore seek the pleasure of his Lord
in everything he does and thus follow in the footsteps of Abraham
and fashion his life according to what the Prophet has been asked
to say.

> (31) My prayers, my sacrifice, my life and my death are all for
>   Allah, the Lord of the worlds; no associates has He and
>   this am I commanded and I am the first of those who
>   submit. (vi. 163-164)

In fact, the very name Muslim signifies one who is entirely
resigned to God and acts according to the will of his Lord. That
is the highest goal of human existence but by no means easily
attainable as Iqbal has expressed it in a couplet:

> To enter into Islam is to step on the altar of love for being
> sacrificed?
>
> People think that it is easy to become a Muslim.

V

THE STORY OF THE PROPHET LUT (LOT)

(May peace and the Blessings of God be upon him)

Lot was a contemporary of the Prophet Abraham. He was his nephew and when Abraham left his homeland, Lot also left with him. He was sent as an apostle and warner to the people of Sodom and Gomorrah, cities utterly destroyed for their unspeakable sins. They cannot be exactly located now, but they are supposed to be somewhere in the plains east of the Dead Sea on the road from Arabia as is said in the Qur'an in xv. 76: "And surely it is on a road that still abides."

Lot was a stranger among the people of Sodom. The Qur'an does not mention him as one of their brothers as it speaks of Hud and Salih. From the words of the Qur'an: "Have we not forbidden you from other people" (xv. 70) it appears that he was not permitted to have any strangers under his roof, or give shelter to them, perhaps due to tribal jealousies.

Three evils are ascribed to Lot's people--homosexual inter-course highway robbery, and openly committing evil deeds in their assemblies. The Qur'an makes mention of it in these words: "What! Do you come to the males and commit robbery on the highways and you commit evil deeds in your assemblies?" (xxix. 29)

Lot was sent to these people to reform them. He himself speaks of his mission in these words: "Surely I am a faithful apostle to you. Therefore guard against the punishment of Allah and obey me." (xxvi 162-163)

But with the exception of a few followers no one listened to his admonitions. The crisis came when on learning that some two handsome youths had come to Lot they invaded his house and demanded of·him to deliver up the youths to them. They were destroyed by a volcanic eruption accompanied by an earthquake, and Lot and his followers were saved.

I. The Bible Accuses Lot

Lot is one of those prophets who have been maligned not only in Rabbinical literature but also in the Bible. Lot was considered a righteous servant of God by Abraham (Genesis, 18: 23) and by saving Lot God has shown that He too regarded Lot as a righteous man. But a little further on in the same chapter we are told that Lot was guilty of incestuous intercourse with his daughters, a fact so inconsistent with righteousness. In Genesis, 19: 31-35, it is stated:

> And the firstborn (daughter of Lot) said unto the younger, Our father is old and there is not a man on the earth to come in unto us after the manner of all the earth: come, let us make our father drink wine, and we will lie with him, that we may preserve seed of our father. And they made their father drink wine that night: and the firstborn went in.
>
> ...And it came to pass on the morrow, that the firstborn said to the younger, Behold, I lay yesternight with my father: let us make him drink wine this night also; and go thou in, and lie with him, that we may preserve seed of our father. And they made their father drink wine that night also: and the younger arose, and lay with him. (Genesis, 19: 31-35)

Such is the abominable fabrication against this holy Prophet of God and his daughters. Is it not strange that a book that contains such filthy stories about the chosen servants of God should pass for Holy Scripture, and yet the adverse critics of the Qur'an have the cheek to assert that the Holy Qur'an is inspired by the stories of the Jewish scripture and that the stories of the prophets as given in the Qur'an are borrowed from such obscene literature?

II. The Story as Told in the Qur'an

The story of Lot is told in various ways under different contexts by the Qur'an in not less than a dozen places. But we shall quote only a few to avoid repetition, bringing out important aspects of the story:

(1) And Lut was most surely of the apostles. (xxxvii. 133).

(2) (Lut said:) Surely I am a faithful apostle to you. Therefore

guard against the punishment of Allah and obey me. And I do not ask you any reward for it. My reward is only with the Lord of the worlds. (xxvi. 162-164)

(3) As for Lut, We gave him wisdom and knowledge...and We took him into Our mercy. Surely he was of the good. (xxi. 74-75)

(4) And We sent Lut, when he said to his people: What! Do you commit an indecency which no one in the world has done before you. You come to men with lust instead of women; any you are an extravagant folk. And the answer of his people was no other than that they said (one to another): Turn them out of your town; surely they are a people who seek to purify themselves. (vii. 80-82)

(5) They said: If thou desist not, O Lut, thou shalt surely be of those who are expelled. He said: My Lord! Deliver me and my followers from what they do. Surely I am of those who abhor utterly their doings. (xxvi. 157-159)

III. The Guests of Abraham and Lot

(6) He (Ibrahim) asked: What is your business then, O messengers? They said: Surely we are sent towards a guilty people, except Lut's followers. We will indeed deliver them all except his wife. We ordained that she shall surely be of those who remain behind. (xv. 57-60)

(7) And when Our messengers came to Lut, he was distressed and knew not how to protect there. He said: This is a distressful day. And his people came to him rushing towards him and already they did evil deeds. He said: O my people! Here are my daughters--they are purer for you-- Beware of the punishment of Allah and do not disgrace me with regard to my guests. Is there not among you one right-minded man?

They said: Certainly thou knowest that we have no right to thy daughters and well thou knowest what we want. He said: Ah! Would that I had power to resist you. I rather would have recourse to a stronger support (from God). They said: O Lut! We are the messengers of thy Lord. They shall by no means reach thee. So, remove thy followers in a part of the night and let none of you turn back--except thy wife. For, whatsoever befalls them shall before her;[22] surely their appointed time is the morning. Is not the morning nigh? (xi. 77-81)

IV. Lot is Delivered and His People Destroyed

(8) The rumbling overtook them while entering upon the time of sunrise. Thus did We turn it upside down and rained down upon them stones according to what had been decreed. Surely in this are signs for those who examine (and take heed). (xv. 73-75)

(9) So We delivered him and his followers except his wife who was of those who remained behind. And We rained upon them a rain. Consider then what was the end of the guilty. (vii. 83-84)

(10) So We delivered him and his followers, all except an old woman among those who remained behind. Then We utterly destroyed the others and We rained down upon them a rain and evil was the rain on those warned. Most surely there is a sign in this but most of them do not believe. And most surely thy Lord is the Mighty, the Merciful. (xxvi. 170-175)

The story, as well as similar such stories of the people to whom prophets were sent, gives us the assurance that God looks after the righteous and in the end only the wicked are overthrown when the cup of their inequity is full.

---

22. In the Biblical narrative she looks back and is turned into a pillar of salt. The Qur'an does not accept such silly stories Here she is represented as a type of those who lag behind, whose mental and moral attitude in spite of their association with the righteous is to hark back to the glitter of wickedness and sin. The righteous should have one sole objective, the way of God. They should not look behind nor yet to the right or left.

VI

THE STORY OF ISMA'IL (ISHMAEL)

(May peace and the Blessings of God be on him)

Ishmael was the firstborn of son of Abraham. He was born to him in response to his prayers. The Qur'an makes mention of it in these words:

(1) Ibrahim said: My Lord! Grant me of the doers of good deeds. So We gave him the good news of a boy possessing forbearance. (xxxvii. 100-101)

According to the Bible, when Hagar who was an Egyptian princess given as handmaid to Sara, the wife of Abraham, gave birth to Ishmael, she was left in the wilderness of Paran on the instigation of Sara who became jealous of her. To accept this would mean that Abraham committed an act of gross injustice against Hagar and her son, and that Sara, the life comrade of so devoted and faithful a servant of God like Abraham, was no better then an ordinary woman. It was one of the ordeals through which Abraham had to pass that he was commanded to part with his son, the only son born in old age, and his wife Hagar, leaving them at the mercy of the desert in the valley of Batha where now the Ka'bah stands. The existence of the two little hills, Safa' and Marwa, in the vicinity of the Ka'bah now absorbed in the city of Mecca, and the monumental rite of the pilgrimage of running to and fro between these two hills in commemoration of Hagar's anguish for her infant son, who was crying for water (a full account of which is given in the chapter on "Hajj" in our book *Islam in Practical Life*) and the sprouting forth of the spring of Zamzam—all this was a part of the Divine scheme and not the outcome of the petty jealousy of a woman as described by the Bible.

When Ishmael grew up, Abraham was made to undergo another ordeal when he was commanded in a vision to sacrifice his son, and we have shown in the story of Abraham that it was Ishmael and not Isaac, as the Bible would have us believe, whom

Abraham was commanded to sacrifice. The Qur'an described it in these words:

(2) And when he attained to working age with him, he said: O my son! Surely I have seen in a dream that I should sacrifice that. Tell me then what thy opinion is. He said: O my father! Do what thou art commanded; if Allah please, thou wilt find me of the patient ones. So, when they both submitted and he threw him down on his forehead, We called out to him, O Ibrahim! Thou hast indeed shown the truth of thy vision. Surely thus do We reward the doers of good. Most surely this is a manifest trial. And We ransomed him with a great sacrifice (xxxvii. 102-107)

Human sacrifice which was common among ancient people prevailed among the Chaldeans also; it also remained in vogue among the Hindus till a very late date. Abraham's seeing in a vision that he too was sacrificing his son and his preparation to fulfil it literally while showing his complete submission to God refers to the custom of human sacrifice and the Divine commandment to sacrifice an animal in his stead shows God's mercy upon His obedient servants and marks the abolition of the savage custom of human sacrifice. This act of Abraham abolished human sacrifice from among many nations and today more than half the world stands indebted to Abraham and Ishmael for their noble example.

Then we are told that Abraham and Ishmael both engaged themselves in raising the foundations of the Ka'bah on the same spot where once this House of God (Bait-Allah) stood but was no more in use as it lay neglected for centuries, and revived the old rite of pilgrimage to this House (Baitul 'Atiq) as the Qur'an calls it on account of its antiquity.

(3) And When We assigned to Ibrahim the site of the House (saying). Do not associate with Me aught and purify My House for those who make the circuit and stand to pray and bow and prostrate themselves. And proclaim among men the pilgrimage. (xxii. 26-27)

(4) And when Ibrahim and Isma'il raised the foundations of the House, (they prayed): Our Lord! Accept from us: surely Thou art the Hearing, the Knowing.
Our Lord! Make us both submissive to Thee and raise from our offspring a nation submitting to Thee and show us our

ways of devotion and turn to us mercifully. Thou art the
Oft-Returning to mercy, the Merciful. (ii. 127-128)

Ishmael and his mother settled down in the vicinity of the
Ka'bah where in course of time the city of Mecca grew up and
became the centre of devotion for believers in the unity of God.

Through Ishmael the Arab nation came into existence in
fulfilment of the covenant that God had made with Abraham and
his son Ishamel We read in Genesis:

I will make of thee a great nation, and I will bless thee,
and make thy name great; and thou shalt be a
blessing...and in thee shall all families of the earth be
blessed. (12: 2-3)

And he brought him forth abroad, and said, Look now
toward heaven and tell the stars, if thus be able to number
them: and he said unto him, So shall thy seed be. (15:5)

The same promise was again given to Hagar regarding Ishmael
when she conceived him.

And the angel of the Lord said unto her (i.e., Hagar), I
will multiply thy seed exceedingly, the it shall not be
numbered for multitude. (Gen. 16:10)

The covenant was made again with Abraham after Ishmael was
born, while Abraham had no hope of another son nor was there
yet a Divine promise that a son would be born to him from Sara,
the promise contained in Genesis, 15:4 "But he that shall come
forth out of thine own bowels shall be thine heir," having been
fulfilled in birth of Ishmael.

This covenant was renewed with Ishmael after Isaac was
promised: "And as for Ishmael, I have heard thee: Behold, I have
blessed him, and will make him fruitful, and will multiply him
exceedingly: twelve princes shall he beget and I will make him
a great nation." (Gen. 17:20)

The connection of Ishmael's name with Arabia is an
incontrovertible fact, for Kedar, son of Ishmael (Gen. 25: 13), stands
throughout the writings of the Old Testament for Arabia (*vide*
Psalms, 120:5 ; Isa, 42: 11; 50: 7, etc.)

(5) Our Lord! Surely I have settled a part of my offspring in
a valley unproductive of fruit near Thy sacred House; Our
Lord! that they may keep up prayer. Therefor, make the
hearts of some people yearn towards them and provide
them with fruits; haply they might be grateful. (xiv. 37)

This verse corroborates the statement of the Bible that one branch of the descendants of Abraham through Ishmael was settled in the vicinity of the sacred House, the Ka'bah, from where the Ishmaelite Arabs spring up.

The Bible does not recognise Ishmael as a prophet of God, although when Abraham prayed as in Genesis, 17: 18: "O that Ishmael might live before thee." the reply was: "And as for Ishmael, I have heard thee" (Gen. 17:20). This shows that Ishmael grew up in the sight of God as a righteous man and was made a prophet. The Qur'an praised him in these words:

(6) And mention Isma'il in the Book. Surely he was truthful in his promise and he was an apostle and a prophet and he enjoined on his family prayer and almsgiving and was one in whom the Lord was well-pleased. (xix 34-35)

In the Holy Qur'an Ishmael is mentioned by name as a prophet along with other prophets about eight times (*vide* verses ii. 133, 136, 140; iii, 83. iv. 163; vi. 87; xxi. 85 and xxxviii. 48).

Abraham and Ishmael, after rebuilding the Ka'bah, the ancient House of God (Baitul 'Atiq) and proclaiming the pilgrimage to it, prayed to God to raise a prophet from their seed in the following words:

(7) Our Lord! And raise up in them an apostle from among them (i.e., our offspring) who shall recite to them Thy communications and teach them the Book and the wisdom and purify them. Surely Thou art the Mighty, the Wise. (ii. 129)

It is on the basis of this verse that the Prophet speaks of himself as "the prayer of my father Abraham," as reported in the Traditions. The Jews of Medina were quite aware of the advent of this prophet according to the prophecies mentioned in their scriptures, specially the one given in Deut., 18: 15-18 which runs as follows:

The Lord thy God will raise up unto thee a Prophet from the midst of thee, of thy brethren like unto me; unto him ye shall hearken...I will raise them up a Prophet from among their brethren, like unto thee, and will put my words in his mouth; and he shall speak unto them all that I shall command him.

The Qur'an refers to this knowledge of theirs when it says:

(8) Those whom We have given the Book recognise him as

they recognise their sons and a party of them most surely conceal the truth while they know it. (ii. 146)

This is all that we learn from the Qur'an about Ishmael and his discendants which is fully endorsed by the accounts still remaining unaltered in the Old Testament.

VII

THE STORY OF THE PROPHETS ISHAQ (ISAAC) AND YA'QUB (JACOB)

(May peace and the Blessings of God be upon them)

Abraham had two sons. The eldest was Ismael whose story we have given in the last chapter. Isaac was his second son born of Sara his wife.

When Abraham came out of the ordeal of sacrificing his only son Ishmael in implicit obedience to the Divine command, he was rewarded with another son named Isaac.

(1) And We gave him the good news of Ishaq, a prophet among the good ones. (xxxvii. 112)

The Qur'an tells us how this news was imparted to him and his wife Sara.

(2) And his wife was standing by, so, she laughed, then, We gave her the good news of Ishaq and after Ishaq (of a son's son) Ya'qub. She said: O wonder! shall I bear a son when I am an extremely old woman and this my husband an extremely old man? Most surely this is a wonderful thing. They said: Dost thou wonder at Allah's bidding. The mercy of Allah and His blessings are on you, O people of the house. Surely He is Praised, the Glorious. (xi. 71-73)

According to Genesis, 21: 5, Abraham was one hundred years old when Isaac was born to him. But when Ishmael was born to him he was eighty-seven years old. According to the covenant between God and Abraham, Isaac was circumcised when he was eight days old. Previously when the covenant was made Abraham got himself circumcised and Ishmael too was circumcised and this was in obedience to the commandment of God which is stated in Genesis 17: 10 in these words:

This is my covenant, which ye shall keep, between me and you and thy seed after thee; Every male child among you shall be circumcised.

From that time onward circumcision has been the characteristic of the Israelites as well as the Ishmaelites, both of them being the descendants of Abraham.

For the gift of these two sons in spite of his old age Abraham expresses his thanks in these words:

(3) Praise be to Allah Who has given me in old age Isma'il and Ishaq. Most surely my Lord is the Hearer of prayer. (xiv. 39)

When Isaac grew up he was made a prophet and after him his son Jacob was also a prophet. The Qur'an informs us:

(4) We gave to him Ishaq and Ya'qub and each one of them We made a prophet. And We granted to them of Our mercy and We caused them to deserve highest commendations. (xix. 49-50)

(5) And We gave him Ishaq and Ya'qub, a son's son, and We made them all good and We made them leaders who guided people by Our command and We revealed to them the way to do good and keeping us prayer and giving of alms and Us alone did they serve. (xxi. 72-73).

(6) And remember Our servants Ibrahim and Ishaq and Ya'qub, men of might and vision. Surely We purified them with a perfect purification keeping in view the life of the final abode. And most surely they were in Our sight the elect, the best. (xxxviii. 45-46).

(7) And We gave him tidings of the birth of Ishaq, a prophet of the righteous, and We showered Our blessing on him and on Ishaq and of their offspring are some who do good and some who plainly wrong their own selves. (xxxvii. 113)

From the above verses it is quite clear that no only Isaac and Jacob were the chosen servants of God, but some of their descendants also were men of high spiritual status and character. Against these testimonies of integrity and piety the Bible gives a damaging account of these people:

In Genesis 26: 7 it is stated that Isaac was a liar, and a coward and no faith in God's protection:

And the men of the place asked him (Isaac) of his wife; and he said, She is my sister: for he feared to say, She is my wife; lest, said he, the men of the place should kill me for Rebekah; because she was fair to look upon.

A similar lie was attributed to Abraham, his father (see the story of Abraham), twice in the same book and the Holy Qur'an had to refute it. And these are the prophets of the Israelites setting examples of high morals to be emulated by their followers.

And in the story given in Genesis 27: 1-35 not only Jacob is charged for fraudulent behaviour but even Isaac is shown as a simpleton and a man of very poor judgment and his wife Rebekah as an intriguing woman. Here is a gist of what the chapter narrates:

Isaac had two sons, Esau the elder and Jacob the younger. Isaac became old and his eyes became blind. He sent of Esau his firstborn and asked him to take his weapons and bring him some venison and so earn his blessings. But Rebekah the wife of Isaac, who was fond of Jacob, quietly presented Jacob in place of Esau and she put the skins of the kids of the goats upon his hands and upon his neck so that he might appear like Esau if touched by his father. By this fraud Jacob secured the blessings of his father. "And when Esau heard the words of his father he cried with a great and exceeding bitter cry, and said unto his father, Bless me, even me also, O my father. And he said. Thy brother came with subtlety, and had taken away thy blessing."

The story does not end here. In Genesis 29: 11-29, Jacob falls in love with his uncle's younger daughter Rachel. His uncle Laban makes Jacob serve him for seven years on promise to marry Rachel with him. At the end of this period Jacob demands Rachel. "Laban gathered together all the men of the place, and made a feast. And it came to pass in the evening, that he took Leah his elder daughter, and brought her to him; and he went in unto her. And Laban gave unto his daughter Leah Zilpah his maid for a handmaid. And it came to pass that in the morning, behold, it was Leah: and he said to Laban, What is this thou hast done unto me? did not I serve with thee for Rachel? wherefore then hast thou beguiled me? And Laban said, It must not be so done in our country, to give the younger before the firstborn. Fulfil her week, and we will give thee this also for the service which thou shalt serve with me yet seven others years. And Jacob did so, and fulfilled her week; and he gave him Rachel his daughter to wife also. And Laban gave to Rachel his daughter Bilhah his handmaid to be her maid." In this way Jacob not only married two sisters but also got two slave-girls to be his concubines as gift from his father-in-law, Laban.

Likewise a narrative in the same book, chapter 30: 20-10, is given showing Jacob's wives and his wives' female slave competing with one another in begetting children for Jacob, which is far from being decent. In the same chapter Jacob is shown obtaining possession of the flocks of Laban by foul methods. Then in chapter 34 Dinah the daughter of Jacob is shown being raped by Shechem, and the sons of Jacob kill Shechem and his father Hamor in retaliation and kill all their people and take away all their wealth and make all their women and children their slaves. Then in chapter 35: 22 Jacob's son Reuben is shown committing incest with his father's concubine Bilhah. The story of Judah the son of Jacob described in chapter 38 committing incest with his own daughter-in-law Tamar is another loathsome tale which can be read in the story of Joseph given in the Bible.

These are only a few of the filthy account given in the Bible about the prophets and their sons and daughters and yet this book is called the *Holy* Bible. May God protect us from attributing such abominable fabrications against His chosen servants. More about Jacob will be found in the story of Joseph which follows.

VIII

THE STORY OF THE PROPHET
YUSUF (JOSEPH)

(May Peace and the Blessings of God be upon him)

Joseph was the son of Jacob otherwise called Israel and the grandson of Isaac the son of Abraham. Almost all the incidents connected with the life of Joseph as described in the Qur'an depict in a parallel manner the dealings of the enemies of the Prophet with him at Mecca and his dealings with them. Unlike the stories of all other prophets the story of Joseph is narrated continuously in one place in the chapter entitled "Yusuf". With the exception of a few Jewish Rabbis who lived in Mecca the story of Joseph was quite unfamiliar to the Arabs. On the instigation of these Rabbis the idolatrous Arabs threw a challenge to the Prophet to tell them how the Israelites came to live in Egypt so that they might test the truth of his claim to divine inspiration. It is probably on this account that the story is given in a single chapter with the opening words:

(1) We narrate unto thee (O Muhammad) the most beautiful of narratives by revealing to thee this Qur'an though before this thou wert certainly of the unaware ones (xii. 3)

and after narrating the whole story the Qur'an concludes in these words:

(2) This is of the announcements of the things unseen which We reveal unto thee and thou wast not with them when they resolved upon their plans and were scheming against him (xii. 102)

referring indirectly to the resolutions of the Quraish and their plans of either killing the Prophet or banishing him or imprisoning him repeating the very ideas which the brothers of Joseph expressed (verses 9 and 10 of this chapter) in order to get rid of him.

The Qur'an does not narrate stories for the sake of giving

my Lord is Forgiving, Merciful.

And the King said: Bring him to me that I may attach him to my person. When he had spoken with him he said: Surely from this day thou shalt be with us invested with rank and trust. Then he (Yusuf) said: Place me in authority over the store-house of the land, surely I am a good custodian, knowing well my duties.

Thus did We give to Yusuf power in the land--he had mastery in it whatever he liked. We bestow Our favours on whom We please and We do not waste the reward of those who do good. And certainly the reward of the Hereafter is much better for those who believe and have regard for their duty. (xii. 43-57)

The version of the Bible in respect of this part of the story is full of repetitions and the whole of chapter 41 is devoted to such details which are redundant and therefore we have omitted to quote this chapter verbatim, but the points which are differently reported are noted below. We refer the readers for fuller information to Genesis, chapter 41 in the Bible.

In the Bible Joseph is brought out of the prison on the instance of the butler to interpret the dream of Pharaoh and after his interpretation he is appointed as the deputy of Pharaoh, but there is no mention of Joseph's being cleared of the charge for which he was imprisoned. The butler could have spoken of Joseph in terms which establish the innocence of Joseph and vindicate his character before the king and Potiphar and other courtiers. He does nothing of the kind in the Bible and yet for a mere interpretation of a dream he is given the kingly authority of Pharaoh in the land-- a thing which is beyond credulity.

But the Qur'an takes up such instances which bear some spiritual lessons instead of indulging itself in such details which have no bearing of any importance on the main theme of the story. It will be seen from the narrative as given in the Qur'an that on hearing the dream of the king and finding no interpretation coming forth from the astrologers of the court the butler remembers Joseph, but as the case of Pharaoh's dream which could not be interpreted by any would be of great consequence, he does not at once mention Joseph's name but first takes the precaution to ascertain if Joseph could solve the mystery. He therefore repairs to the prison, and on getting a satisfactory explanation, he then tells the king about Joseph.

It is then that Joseph is summoned. But instead of feeling happy at his release and responding readily to the call he refuses to leave the prison until he has his innocence established beyond all doubt. Here is a lesson to note that a man's honour has a greater value than all worldly prosperity. If by a stroke of luck one gains a high position with a stigma associated with his name, it is not a thing worth having. Therefore an inquiry is held. The society women bear evidence and even Potiphar's wife makes a confession (verse 51) and the innocence of Joseph is established. Mark the words. in which he expresses his own weakness and acknowledges the mercy of God on His faithful servants: "I do not exculpate myself; most surely the heart of man is prone to evil except such of those on whom my Lord hath mercy; for surely my Lord is Forgiving, Merciful" words becoming the mouth of a man of God! The animal in man again and again commands him to do evil, but he refrains from doing it, being involved as it were in a great struggle to get out of the power of evil. This gives him the strength of conscience and puts him on the path of rectitude, and leads him further on to a stage where he finds perfect peace. Such are the people on whom the Lord hath mercy.

Then the king interviews him and gets so good an impression of him that he wishes to make him his trusted and honourable courtier. In the Bible the king offers him to become his deputy but in the Qur'an Joseph himself offers his service saying with full confidence: "Place me in authority over the store-houses of the land, surely I am a good custodian, knowing well my duties." Here again is a lesson which tells us that in the interest of good government it is necessary that those who are rightly confident of their own aptitudes should offer themselves without hesitation for job in which they can be of real service to their country.

With the appointment of Joseph the Divine purpose is made clear in these words: "And thus did We give to Yusuf power in the land-he had mastery in it whatever he liked. We bestow Our favours or whom We please and We do not waste the reward of those who do good. And certainly the reward of the Hereafter is much better for those who believe and have regard for their duty." (verses 56:57). In vain would one search the Bible narrative for such spiritual lessons.

After the exaltation of Joseph the Qur'an omits the details of how he stored up corn and how he helped the famine-stricken people as all that information has no bearing on the main theme of the story. It goes straight to mention about the coming of Joseph's brethren and what happened to them and how, ultimately, Jacob goes and settles down in the land of Egypt with all his family. But in the narration of these incidents the Qur'anic version differs in many aspects from the version of the Bible.

We shall deal only with those differences along with the narrative of the Qur'an and show that the Qur'anic·version is more logical, psychological, and to the point, whereas the account given in the Bible is boring, superfluous and in places self-contradictory.

VII. Joseph's Helps His Brothers

(9) And Yusuf's brothers came and presented themselves before him and he knew them while they did not recognise him. And when he furnished them with their provision he said: Bring to me a brother of yours from your father. Do you not see that I give full measure and that I am the best of hosts? But if you do not bring him to me you shall have no measure of corn from me nor shall you come near me.

They said: We will try to make his father listen to us in respect of him and will surely do it.

And he said to his servants: Put their money into their bags that they may perceive it when they go back to their families, so that they may come back.

So when they returned to their father they said: O our father The measure is withheld from us unless we take our brother. So, send with us our brother so that we may get the measure and we will most surely take care of him.

He said: Shall I trust you with respect to him except as I trusted you with respect to his brother before? But Allah is the best guardian and He is the most Merciful of the merciful ones.

And when they opened their baggage they found their money returned to them. They said: O our father! What more can we desire? Here is our money returned to us and we will bring corn for our family and guard our brother

and will have in addition the measure of a camel load;
this is but a small quantity.
He said: I will by no means send him with you until you
give me a firm covenant in Allah's name and you will most
certainly bring him back to me unless you are hemmed
in and made powerless. And when they gave him their
covenant he said: Let Allah be the witness over what we
say. And he said: O my sons! Do not all enter by one gate
and enter by different gates, but I cannot avail you aught
against Allah with my advice. The decision rests with Allah
alone. On Him do I rely and on Him let those who are
reliant reply.
And when they had entered as their father had bidden
them it did not profit them in the least against the plan
of Allah but it only served to satisfy a desire of Ya'qub's
heart, and surely he was possessed of knowledge which
We had given him but most men have not that knowledge.
(xii. 58-68)

VIII. The Youngest Brother

(10) And when they came into Yusuf's presence he lodged his
own brother with himself saying: I am thy brothers.
Therefore grieve not at what they do.
At length when he furnished them with their provisions,
a drinking cup was placed in his brother's bag. Then a
crier cried out: O caravan! You are most surely thieves.
They returned back to them and said: What is it that you
miss?
They said: We miss the King's drinking cup and he who
shall bring it shall have a.camel load and I pledge himself
responsible for it.
They said: By Allah, you know for certain that we have
not come to make mischief in the land, and we are not
thieves. They said: But what shall be the penalty for it if
you are found liars? They said: The penalty for it is that
the person in whose bag it is found shall be given unto
you in satisfaction for it. Thus do we punish the unjust?
Then he began the search with their sacks before the sack
of his brother, then he brought it out from his brother's

sack. Thus did We furnish Yusuf with a stratagem, for it was not lawful that he should take his brother under king's law except that Allah willed it so. We raise the degrees of whomsoever We please and the All-Knowing one is above everyone possessed of knowledge.

They said: If he steal, a brother of his did indeed steal before. But Yusuf kept it concealed in his heart and did not disclose it to them. He said to himself: You are in a worse condition and Allah knows best what you state. They said: O chief! He has a father, a very old man, therefore take one of us in his stead. Surely we perceive thou art a beneficent person. He said: Allah forbid us that we should seize other than him with whom we found our property, for them, most surely we would be unjust. (xii. 67-79)

IX. Joseph Discloses His Identity to His Brothers

(11) Then when they despaired of him, they retired conferring privately together. The eldest of them said: Do you not know that your father took from you a covenant in Allah's name and how you fell short of your duty with respect to Yusuf before. Therefore I will by no means depart from this land until my father permits me or Allah decide for me and He is the best of judges. Go back to your father and say: O our father! Surely thy son committed theft and we do not bear witness except to what we have known and we could not keep watch over the unseen. And inquire in the town in which we were and the caravan with which we proceeded and most surely we are truthful.

He (Ya'qub) said: Nay, your minds have made this thing seem pleasant to you. So patience is most fitting for me. May be Allah may restore them all to me. Surely He is the Knowing, the Wise.

And he turned away from them and said: O how I am grieved for Yusuf! And his eyes became white with grief on account of suppressing his sorrow. They said: Thou wilt not cease to think of Yusuf until thy health is ruined or until thou art of those who perish. He said: I only complain of my grief and sorrow to Allah and I know from Allah

what you do not know O my sons! Go, and seek tidings
of Yusuf and his brother and despair not of Allah's mercy.
Surely none despairs of Allah's mercy except the
unbelieving people.

And when they came back unto Yusuf's presence they said:
O chief! Distress has afflicted us and our family and we
have brought scanty money; so give us full measure and
be charitable to us; surely Allah rewards the charitable.
He said: Do you know how you dealt with Yusuf and his
brother not knowing what you were doing? They said:
Canst thou indeed be Yusuf? He said: I am Yusuf and this
my brother. Allah has indeed been Gracious to us. Surely
whose feareth Allah and endureth is rewarded, for surely
Allah doth not waste the reward of those who do good.
They said: By Allah: Now hath he chosen thee over us
and we were indeed sinners. He said: There shall be no
reproof against you this day. Allah may forgive you and
He is the most Merciful of the mercifuls. Take this my shirt
and cast it on my father's face and he will recover his sight
and come to me with all your families. (xii. 80-93)

Now, instead of quoting the version of the Bible regarding these
incidents we are quoting only those portions which are different
from the version of the Qur'an to avoid uncalled-for details, boring
repetitions, and superfluous material, so that our readers may be
able to form their estimations of the two narratives. Chapters 42
to 45 of the Book of Genesis can be studied with advantage for
this comparison.

The Bible says:

(1) And Joseph saw his brethren, and he knew them, but made
himself strange to them, and spake roughly to them; and
he said unto them, Whence come ye? and they said, From
the land of Canaan to buy food. And Joseph knew his
brethren, and they knew not him. And Joseph remembered
the dreams which he dreamed of them, and said unto
them, Ye are spies; to see the nakedness of the land ye
are come. And they said unto him, Nay, my lord, but to
buy food are thy servants come. We are all one man's sons;
we are true men, thy servants are no spies. And he said
unto them, Nay, but to see the nakedness of the land ye

are come. And they said, Thy servants are twelve brethren, the sons of one man in the land of Canaan; and behold the youngest it is this day with our father, and one is not. And Joseph said unto them, That is it that I spake unto you saying, Ye are spies: hereby ye shall be proved: By the life of Pharaoh ye shall not go forth hence, except your youngest brother come hither. Send one of you, and let him fetch your brother, and ye shall be kept in prison, that your words may be proved, whether there be any truth in you: or else by the life of Pharaoh surely ye are spies. And he put them all together into ward three days. And Joseph said unto them the third day, This do, and live; for I fear God: If ye be true men, let one of your brethren be bound in the house of your prison: go ye, carry corn for the famine of your houses: but bring your youngest brother unto me, so shall your words be verified, and ye shall not die. And they did so (Gen. 42: 7-20).

(2) And he said unto his brethren, My money is restored; and lo, it is even in my sack: and their heart failed them, and they were afraid, saying one to another, What is the that God has done unto us? (ibid., 28).

(3) And it came to pass as they emptied their sacks, that behold, every man's bundle of money was in his sack and when both they and their father saw the bundles of money, they were afraid (ibid., 35).

In the Bible the brothers of Joseph are condemned by him as spies and treated roughly and put into prison for three days and one of them is taken as hostage and their money is hidden in their sacks and all this is done so that they may out of fear bring Joseph's own brother Benjamin to Egypt. But the Qur'an tells us that Joseph treated his brothers very generously, saying: "Do you not see that I give full measure and that I am the best of hosts?" And when they found their money in their baggage they were not afraid but were impressed with the generosity of their host and pleaded strongly before their father to send Benjamin with them, It is a psychological truth that kindness is a more powerful incentive than force to get things accomplished and Joseph employed it and left no room for his brothers to entertain any ill-feeling against him even after his discovery.

In the Bible narrative, after the episode of the cup, Joseph discloses himself to his brothers being overwhelmed with compassion on hearing the speech of Judas (chapt. 45: 1-5) but the Qur'an makes the plot of the story more impressively deep. Judas stays back and sends his brothers to his father to relate the episode of the cup. Jacob blames them in exactly the same words in which he had blamed them when they had brought to him Joseph's shirt with false blood on it. This incident gives him a renewed hope of meeting Joseph, for, he says: "May be Allah restore them all to me. Surely He is the Knowing, the Wise."

His mouring for Joseph makes him nearly blind and his son blame him for continuing to mourn for Joseph so long after he had perished. But Jacob's hopes grew greater Still. He says: "I only complain of my grief and sorrow to Allah and I know from Allah what you do not know. O my sons! Go and seek tidings of Yusuf and his brother and despair not of Allah's mercy. Surely none despairs of Allah's mercy except the unbelieving people." This shows that Jacob had a true prophet's faith in the Divine promise given to him about Joseph and he knew by revelation that Joseph was alive.

Here it should be noted that when Jacob agrees to send Benjamin with his brothers the Bible makes him say:

And God Almighty give you mercy before the man, that he may send away your other brother, and Benjamin (Gen. 43: 14).

But according to Genesis 37: 33-34, Jacob believes that Joseph is without doubt rent into pieces. "And Jacob rent his clothes, and put sackcloth upon his loins, and mourned for his son many days." This is one of the examples of several inconsistencies that we find in the narrative of the Bible.

In Genesis 45: 4 Joseph tells his brothers: "I am Joseph your brother, whom ye sold into Egypt," whereas in Genesis 37: 36 it is said: "And the Midianites sold him into Egypt unto Potiphar, an officer of Pharaoh's, and captain of the guard." This is another example of the inconsistencies of the Bible. Again in Genesis 44: 1, it is stated that Joseph ordered his steward to "put every man's money in his sack's mouth." When the sacks were searched for the cup the money must also have been discovered and the brothers could have remonstrated that whoever was responsible for putting the money there was also responsible for placing the cup in the sack and could have easily exonerated themselves of the charge of theft.

But they did not do it. According to the version of the Qur'an, the money was not placed in the sacks along with the cup and, therefore,, the brothers had no plea to absolve Benjamin from theft. At the same time as Benjamin was aware of Joseph's identity before the incident of the cup took place, he was not at all perturbed at the discovery of the cup in his sack, for he was already cautioned about it by Joseph himself in these words: "I am thy brother; therefore grieve not at what they do." (xii. 69).

Though these instances are very petty, yet these are proofs of the fact that the Bible is based on folklore and the Qur'an on divine inspiration.

X. Israel Goes to Egypt

And now to finish the story let us go back again to the Qur'an:
(12) And when the caravan left Egypt their father said: Most
surely I scent the perfume of Yusuf. Nay think me not
a dotard. They said: By Allah! thou· art in thy old
aberration. Then when the bearer of the good news came,
he cast it (the shirt) on his face and he forthwith regained
his clear sight. He said: Did I not say to you that I know
from Allah what you do not know. They said: O father!
Ask forgiveness of our faults for us. Surely we were
sinners. He said: Soon shall I ask for your forgiveness from
my Lord. Surely He is the Forgiving, the Merciful. Then
when they came in to Yusuf, he took his parents to lodge
with him and said: Enter safe into Egypt if Allah please.
And raised his parents upon the throne and they made
obeisance to him and he said: O my father! This is the
fulfilment of my vision of old. My Lord has indeed made
it to be true and He was indeed kind to me when He
brought me forth from prison and brought you all from
the desert even after Satan has sown dissensions between
me and my brothers. Surely my Lord is Benignant to whom
He pleases. Surely He is the Knowing, the Wise.
My Lord! Thou hast indeed given me of the kingdom and
taught me of the interpretation of dreams. Originator of

the heavens and the earth! Thou art my guardian in this world and the Hereafter. Make me die a Muslim and join me with the righteous. (xii. 94-101)

Now turning to the Bible we find in Genesis 46 that Jacob takes all the members of his family with him to Egypt. Here an unnecessary lengthy list of the names of all the members of the family is given. In the way the God Israel says: "I will go down with thee into Egypt; and I will also surely bring thee again" (Gen. 46: 4). But Jacob dies in Egypt and only his corpse is brought to Canaan (Gen. 50:. 13) which is again inconsistent with the promise of the God of Israel.

The meeting of Joseph with his father and his setting them in the land of Goshan, with the permission of Pharaoh until the death of Jacob and the mourning of the Egyptians and the Israelites and taking the corpse of Jacob to Cannan for burial, is described at great length in the Bible as a boring narrative of very little consequence to the main theme of the story.

The Qur'an, on the other hand, after describing how Jacob felt overjoyed on the recovery of his beloved sons and how he regained his lost sight by the miracle of the short and how Joseph received his parents,[24] and his brothers and how they made obeisance to him, thereby fulfilling the dream which he dreamed in the beginning of the story, ends the story of Joseph with his prayer to God for bringing all his troubles to a happy ending.

In fact, the interest of the story terminates at the termination of the troubles of the family of Israel and therefore the Qur'an's ending is more appropriate and psychological than what we find in the Bible with its addition of four more chapters. The difference of the two narratives can be summed up as the difference between secular and sacred history, between a record of the past events based on mere hearsay and great spiritual lessons for the future.

---

24. The Christian critic is very quick in finding fault with the Qur'an saying that Joseph's Mother Rachel had long been dead, but the Prophet makes both his parents make obeisance to Joseph to bring the event into strict accordance with the prediction of the dream But they forget that Leah was Rachel's elder sister and a wife of Jacob (Gen 29:16-28). The fact that Rachel was dead in no way contradicts this statement because Leah would be Jospeh's mother in both capacities as his mother's sister and his father's wife.

XI. In the Story of Joseph is a Prophetic Announcement of the Prophet's Success

It should be borne in mind that in the Qur'anic story of Joseph is related the story of the Prophet Muhammad himself as it is told in the beginning that "Certainly in the story of Yusuf and his brothers there are signs for the inquirers" (xii. 7). Such is also the end. After being raised to the highest dignity in the land Joseph prays to God, and then follow the memorable words:

(13) This is of the announcements relating to the unseen which We have revealed to thee and thou wast not with them when they resolved upon their affair and they were devising plans. (xii. 102)

These were clearly the plans which the Prophet's enemies were devising to put an end to his life and get rid of him and he is told. that their plan would fail and they would come to him as Joseph's brothers came to Joseph asking pardon for their cruelty to him, and meeting with the magnanimous response of which history does not offer another instance, would be reconciled to him. When the Prophet on the conquest of Mecca took hold of the two sides of the door of the Ka'bah and said to the Quraish: "What treatment do you expect from me after all that you have done to me and my followers?" They said: "We hope for good from a noble brother and the son of a noble brother." Then he said: "I say to you as my brother Joseph said:

There shall be no reproof against you this day. Allah may forgive you and He is the most Merciful of the merciful ones (xii. 92)

The comparison of the two narratives is over. Now our readers can judge for themselves how far removed from the truth are Noldeke's remarks about the stories of the Qur'an.

No doubt, the story is similar to but not identical with the Biblical story. But the atmosphere is wholly different. The Biblical story is a folk-tale based upon the real story having no morality in it. Its tendency is to exalt the clever and financial-minded Jew against the Egyptian and to explain certain ethnic and tribal peculiarities in later Jewish history. The Qur'anic story, on the other hand, is less a narrative than a highly spiritual sermon, explaining the seeming contradictions of life, the enduring nature of virtue in a world full of flux and change and the marvellous working of

God's eternal purpose in His plan as unfolded to us on the wide canvas of history.

XII. Lessons from the Story of Joseph

In the course of our comparative evaluation of the incidents of the two narratives, we have touched upon the various spiritual lessons one can derive from the story of Joseph. But here are some more special morals that can be derived from the above story.

(1) The dreams of the righteous prefigure great events while the dreams of the futile are mere idle fantasies. Even things that happen to us are often like dreams. The righteous man receives disasters and reverses not with blasphemies against God but with humble devotion, seeking to ascertain his will, nor does he receive good fortune with arrogance but an opportunity for doing good to friends and foes alike and show his gratitude to Him.

(2) Whatever happens is the result of God's will and plan and He is Good and Wise and He knows all things. Therefore in all the vicissitudes of our life we must lay our trust in Him and do our duty with a firm belief in His goodness and wisdom. He is sure to lead us to success through all our adversities if we are faithful to Him.

(3) In the episode of the woman's love affair with Joseph is a lesson for the weak minded. Joseph was human after all and the passionate love of the woman and her beauty placed a great temptation in his path. But he had a sure refuge--his faith in God. His eyes saw something that the woman's eyes blinded by passion could not see. She thought no one saw them when the doors were closed. He knew that God was there as everywhere else. That made him strong and proof against temptation. A strong belief in the Omnipresence and the Omniscience of God is a sure refuge against all the onslaughts of vice. But the credit of being saved from sin is due not to our weak earthly nature but to God alone. We can only try like Joseph to be true and sincere. God will purify us and save us from all that is wrong. Tempted but true we rise above ourselves. Mark the prayer of Joseph: "My Lord! the prison-house is preferable to me to that to which they invite me; if Thou turn not away their snares from me I may perchance yearn towards them out of my youthful folly and become one of the unwise." Like a true man of God, Joseph takes refuge in God. He knows the

weakness of human nature. He would not put faith in his own strength against the whole assault of evil. He will rely on God to turn the evil away from him and praise Him along for any success he achieves in his fight with it. It is only the ignorant who do not understand man's weakness and God's power.

(4) In the imprisonment of Joseph may appear to superficial minds that virtue is not rewarded, but always the plan of God works out its own beneficent purposes. It was destined through this incident that he should get in touch with Pharaoh in order to work out the salvation of Egypt. A man of faith in God should therefore be fortitudinous in whatever happens to him, for no one knows what destiny lies in store for him. Here is an example of the wonderful working of Divine Providence. The boy whom his jealous brothers got rid of and who was sold into slavery for a miserable price became the most trusted dignitary in a foreign land and chief minister in one of the greatest empires of the world of that day. And this, not for himself only, but of his family, for the world at large, and for that noble example of righteousness and strenuous service which he was to set for all time. To the righteous, whatever rewards, If any, that come in this world are welcome for the opportunities of service which they open out. But the true and the best reward is in the Hereafter.

(5) Joseph's shirt plays an important role in the story. His brothers smear the shirt with false blood as evidence of his death but fail to convince his father. Again it is the shirt rent from behind that established the innocence of Joseph in the woman's love affair, and 'once again it is the shirt of Joseph that brings sight to his father's eyes. Amongst the miracles wrought by the prophets that of the shirt is only an insignificant portent but a little thought into this will reveal some important truths. The shirt on account of its proximity with the person of the prophet was able to produce so grand an effect as the restoration of a lost sight, the relic of a hair from the body of the Prophet Muhammad (may peace and blessings of God be upon him) which has been preserved in many a Muslim family should be a much more significant portent than the shirt and should possess even greater effects. Is it not said in the Qur'an that "Allah is not going to chastise them while thou art among them" (viii. 33) and, therefore, wherever there is this relic, that place is sure to be secure from calamities. For those who criticise people who pay reverence to such relics as superstitious, here is

food for thought. Same was the case with "The Ark of the Lord" (Tabut-i-Sakina) in which the relics of the prophets of Israel were preserved and whose miraculous powers the Bible gives long accounts.

Before we end this chapter, one misunderstanding among the Muslims must be cleared. There is a popular tradition that the name of the wife of Potiphar who attempted to seduce Joseph was Zulaikha and though she failed in her attempt to make Joseph yield to her carnal desires, later on she repented and her earthly passion grew into a pure spiritual doting for Joseph and ultimately Joseph married her. The Qur'an, the Bible and the Traditions of the Prophet are all silent in this respect and even those commentators of the Qur'an who are notorious for inserting spurious tales of the Jews into their commentaries have not given any clue to the sources from which this romance is derived. At first Firdausi, the Persian poet, tried to weave a romance out of the story of Joseph and the wife of Potiphar and later Jami, another Persian poet, tried his hand at it. There is a good German translation of this romantic poem of Jami by Rozenzweig and an English Translation by R.T. H. Griffith published in 1881. But the things mentioned in Jami's story are the product of poetic imagination with no basis in its version of the Qur'an or Hadith.

IX

THE STORY OF THE PROPHET SHU'AIB

(May peace and blessings of God be on him)

The Prophet Shu'aib was a descendant of Abraham in the fourth generation. Madyan or Midian was the name of Abraham's son by his wife Keturah (Gen. 25: 2). A city of the same name grew upon the coast of the Red Sea, south-east of Mount Sinai where some of his descendants must have settled.

Shu'aib belongs to Arab tradition rather than to Jewish tradition to which he is unknown. His identification with Jethro of the Bible, the father-in-law of Moses, has no warrant. Thee is no similarity either in names or incident and there are chronological difficulties also. If Shu'aib was in the fourth generation from Abraham, it would be impossible for him to be a contemporary of Moses who came many centuries later. The mere fact that Jethro was a Midianite is slender ground for his identification with Shu'aib. As the Midianites were mainly nomads, we need not be surprised than their destruction in one or two of their settlements did not affect the peculiarities of their life in their wandering tribal sections in other regions Shu'aib's mission was apparently in one of the settled towns of the Midianties which was completely destroyed by an earthquake.

If this happened in the country after Abraham, there is no difficulty in supposing that they were again a numerous tribe four or five centuries later in the time of Moses. For, we find in the Bible that their principal territory in the time of Mose was in the north-east of the Sinai peninsula. Under Moses the Israelites waged a war of extermination against them. They slew the kings of Midian, slaughtered all their males, burnt their cities and castles and captured their cattle (Numbers 31: 7-11). This sounds like total extermination. Yet a few generations afterwards they were so powerful that the Israelites, for their sins, were delivered into the captivity of the Midianites for seven years. "Both the Midianites and their camels were without number and the Israelites hid from them in dens, caves, and strongholds" (Judges 7: 1-6). Gideon destroyed them again (Judges 7: 1-25) about two centuries after Moses, this and the previous destruction under Moses were local and mention no town of the Midianites.

So, we need not be misled by the narrative of the Old Testament where the Midianites are frequently mentioned. The story of Shu'aib and his people has nothing to do with Midianites of the Bible, and the earthquake that destroyed Midian must have happened about a century after Abraham.

Shu'aib is mentioned as being sent to Midian as well as to the dwellers of the wood[25] who, being in all particulars almost identical with the people of Midian, may be taken to be the same people.

Midian was on the commercial highway of Asia between Egypt and Assyria and Babylonia. The sins of the Midianites as expressed in the Qur'an, were: (1) giving short measures and weights; (2) a general form of fraud depriving people of their rightful dues: (3) producing mischief and disorder where peace and order had been established; (4) not content with upsetting settled life, taking to highway robbery literally as well as (5) metaphorically, in two ways, namely, cutting of people from access to the worship of God and abusing religion and piety for crooked purpose. Now read what the Qur'an says:

---

25. The Qur'an calls them Ashab-ul-Aikah which means companions of the wood, and these are indentified with the people of Midian, the location of hich, as pointed out above, was on the coast of the Red Sea, in the neighbourhood of the gulf of 'Aqabah But the whole valley of 'Aqabah is a bleak stony desert with hardly a tree to relieve the monotony of the vast stretch except a few studented junipers and palm trees growing scantily here and there where some brackish water is gathered in a pool To say that in such a place there once existed a forest would seem incredible. Even the early Muslim geographers are silent about the forest existing in this region. Consequently till now the commentators of the Qur'an have sheltered themselves behind the explanation that 'Aikah was a proper name of a long lost town in that region. But now Mr. Burton, the author of *The Gold Mines of Midian*, on the authority of Greek geographers has stated that this region was one overgrown with trees so dense thet it represented all the typical fauna of the forest, For further details see pages 179-80 and chapter 88 of Burton's book Here is one more instance which shows that the informaion given in the Qur'an is no piece of plagiarism of the Bible

(1) And We sent to Midian their brother Shu'aib. He said: O
my people! Serve God. You have no other god than Him.
Now hath a clear sign come to you from your Lord. give
therefore the full in measure and weight, nor withhold
from people the things that are their due, and commit no
disorder in the land after once it has been set in order;
this will be the best course for you if you are believers.
And lie not in ambush by every road in a menacing way,
nor mislead him who believeth in God from his way, nor
mislead him who believeth in God from his way, nor seek
to make it crooked. And remember, when you were few,
how He multiplied you and, behold, what hath been the
end of those who made mischief. (vii. 85-86).

Shu'aib began his argument with faith in God as the source
of all virtue and ended it with destruction as the result of all sin.

(2) And if there is a party among you who believes in the
message with which I am sent, and a party which does
not believe, then wait steadfastly until Allah shall judge
between us, for He is the best of judges.

The chiefs of his people with puffed-up pride said: We will
certainly banish thee, O Shu'aib, and thy fellow-believers
from our city unless ye shall come back to our ways of
life. What! said he, even though we abhor it? We shall
indeed be inventing a lie against Allah if we returned to
your ways after Allah hath rescued us from it, nor can
we return to it unless it be the will of Allah our Lord.
Our Lord embraceth all things in His ken. We rely on Allah
our Lord. O our Lord, decide Thou between us and our
people, for the best to decide art Thou. (vii. 87-89).

The gentle persuasive arguments of Shu'aib fell on hard hearts.
When courtesy and a plea for toleration are pitted against bigotry,
no room is left for logic. "Come back to our ways of life" to the
ways of injustice, oppression, high-handedness to the poor and
the weak, and fraud under cover of religion, and so on. If not,
"Our you go in disgrace" was the demand. The answer of the
righteous was threefold: (i) Should we practise what we detest?
(ii) Should we lie against or conscience and our God after once
knowing the truth; (iii) we leave the matter with God and we rely
upon His guidance, for He knows what is best for us.

Then the righteous turn to God in earnest prayer Whose decision is free from error and the imperfections of all human judgment, and they whose motives are pure have nothing to fear in the appeal to Him.

(3) And the chief of the people who believed not said: If you follow Shu'aib, you shall then surely be ruined.

An earthquake, therefore, took them unawares and they lay prostrate in their homes before the morning. Those who rejected Shu'aib became as though they had never dwelt in the homes where they had flourished, they who had treated Shu'aib as an impostor were the losers.

So, Shu'aib left them saying: O my people! I did convey to you the message of my Lord and I counselled you aright, but how should I be grieved for a people who refused to believe. (vii. 90-93).

The answer of the unbelievers is characteristic. As all their bribes and subtleties failed, they resorted to threats which are worse than the argument of the stick. "All right!" they say, "there is nothing but ruin before you." That mean that the believers will be persecuted, held up to ridicule, ostracised and prevented from access to all means of honourable livelihood; their families and dependants will be insulted, reviled, and tortured if they could be got into enemy's power and their homes destroyed. But their wicked designs recoil on themselves, and it is the wicked who are ruined and blotted out. That is the Law of God.

The fate of the Midianites is described in the same terms as that of the Thamud.

In another chapter the same story is repeated but from a different angle. There the emphasis is on their treatment of their prophets and here the emphasis is on God's dealing with men and their obstinate ways, thus throwing light on some of the sins of Meccans in the Holy Prophet's time.

(4) They said: O Shu'aib! Does thy religion of prayer command thee that we leave of the worship that our fathers practised or that we leave off doing what we like with our property? Truly thou art the one that forbearth with faults and is right-minded. (xi. 87)

It is the usual way of selfish and material-minded people to scoff at spiritual things like prayer and to hug their own property rights as if there were no other rights greater or more important than that of property. Their remarks here are very sarcastic in calling him the only right-minded man.

Shu'aib's answer is gentle and pursuasive. He appeals to them as man to man. He vision takes in the fate of previous generations who sinned and perished on account of their iniquities. He therefore advises them to repent and ask forgiveness of God.

(5) He said: O my people! Have you considered if I have a clear proof from my Lord and He has given me a goodly sustenance from Himself, and I do not desire that in opposition to you I should betake myself to that which I forbid you, I desire nothing but reform so far as I am able, and with none but Allah is the direction of my affairs to a right issue. On Him do I rely and to Him do I turn. And O my people! Let not opposition to me make you guilty so that there may befall you the like of what befell the people of Nuh or the people of Hud or the people of Salih nor are the people of Lut far off from you. And ask forgiveness of your Lord, and turn to Him; surely my Lord is Merciful, Loving, Kind.

They said: O Shu'aib! We do not understand much of what thou sayest and most surely we see thee to be weak among us and were it not for thy family, we would surely stone thee and thou art not mighty against us.

He said: O my people! Is my family more esteemed by you than Allah? And you neglect Him as a thing cast behind your back. Surely my Lord encompasseth what you do.

And O my people! Act according to your ability; I too am acting. you will come to know soon who it is on whom will light the punishment that will disgrace him and who it is that is a liar. And watch; surely I too am watching with you.

And when Our decree came to pass, We delivered Shu'aib and those who believed with him by mercy from us and the rumbling overtook those who were unjust, so they became motionless bodies in their abodes, as though they had never dwelt in them. Now surely perdition overtook Midian as had perished the Thamud. (xi. 84-95)

(6) Most surely there is a sign in this, but most of them do
    not believe (xxvi. 190).

If the wicked continue to blaspheme and mock, what can the
godly say but this: "Watch and Wait," God's plan works without
fail. "We have faith and we too will watch with you for its
fulfilment."

How exactly these past experiences fit the times of the Holy
Prophet. It is for that analogy and the lesson that the stories of
Noah, Hud, Salih, Lot and Shu'aib are related to us all different
and yet all pointing to the great lesson in Muhammad's life (may
peace and blessings of God be on him).

X

THE STORY OF THE PROPHET YUNUS (JONAH)

(May peace and blessings of God be on him)

The Prophet Yunus otherwise called "Lord of the Fish" (Dhun-Num) and "Companion of the Fish" Sahib-ul-Hut) was sent to Nineveh, the once capital city of Assyria. It is an ancient town which is no longer on the map. Its site is believed to be marked by the two mounds on the left bank of the Tigris opposite the city of Mosul, on the right bank about 230 miles north-north-west of Baghdad. One of the mounds bears the name of "The Tomb of Nabi Yunus". Archaeologists have not yet fully explored its antiquitis. But it is clear that it was an old Sumerian town, perhaps older than 3500 B.C. The first Assyrian Empire under Shalmanesser I about 1300 B.C. was supreme power in western Asia. Babylon, whose tributary Assyria had formerly been, now became tributary to Assyria. The second Assyrian empire arose about 745 B.C. and Sennachrib (705-681) beautified the town with many public works. It was destroyed by the Scythians in 612 B.C. If the date of Jonah were assumed to be about 800 B.C. it would be between the first and the second Assyrian Empire, when the city was nearly destroyed for its sins, but on account of its repentance was given a new lease of glorious life in the second empire. But soon, like Babylon, it become the city of sin and consequently was destroyed by the Scythians. A reference of the fresh lease that was granted to this city and its people is given in the Qur'an in these words:

(1) When they believed, We removed from them the penalty of ignominy in the life of the present and permitted them to enjoy their life for a while. (x. 98).

In this connection it would be noted that Jonah bears a resemblance to the Prophet, as his people also benefited by the warning though after much opposition. Jonah is thus the type of a prophet whose people were dealt with mercifully.

Jonah as a prophet is mentioned along with several other prophets in iv. 163 and vi. 85 but some details of his mission are given in the following passages:

(2) And remember Dhun-Nun when he departed in wrath: he imagined that We had no power over him, but he called out in distress: There is no god but Thou Glory be to Thee; indeed I was of those who do wrong to themselves. So, We listened to him and delivered him distress, and thus do We deliver those who have faith (xxi. 87-88).

(3) And Yunus was most surely of the apostles. When he fled to a ship fully laden, he (agreed to) cast lots and he was (consequently) of those who are cast off. Then a fish drew him with its mouth as he was worthy of blame. He would certainly have remained in its belly (devoured) till the day of resurrection. But We cast him on the naked shore in a state of sickness and We caused to grow over him a spreading plant of the gourd kind. (And when he got well) We sent him (on his mission) to a hundred thousand (men) or more and they believed. So We permitted them to enjoy (Our bounty) for a while. (xxvii. 139-148).

In quotation (2) Jonah is called Dhun-Nun (Lord of the Fish) as he was caught by a fish when he was cost into the sea. When his first warning was not heeded by his people, he invoked God's wrath on the people and departed in wrath from them. But he should have remained with them even under the most discouraging circumstances and relied on the power of God for success. But he went away to the sea and took a boat, but the sailors, after drawing lots, threw him overboard as a man bringing ill-luck in a storm. He was caught by a fish and in extreme distress which he had brought on himself, he called on God, and God the most Gracious forgave him. He was caused to be cast ashore and was given the shelter of a spreading plant, and refreshed and strengthened and was ordered to return to his mission which then prospered. Thus he regained God's pleasure, overcame all his difficulties and realised his hopes by repentance and faith in God and his people also prospered similarly.

The Qur'an does not mention that he was devoured by the fish for the word used here does not necessarily signify the act of devouring but simply that of drawing or taking into the mouth. There is a saying of the Prophet that only his heel was drawn by the fish into its mouth. This is another circumstance wherein the Qur'an disagrees with the Bible wherein it is stated that he remained alive in its belly for three days (see Jonah, I: 17).

When he regained his health, he was ordered by God to go back to his city and fulfil his mission of making the people give up their iniquitous life. The people repented and Nineveh got a new lease of life.

The example of Jonah is quoted in another passage of the Qur'an asking the Prophet to wait and see the result with resignation to the will of God in his persecutions and not to be in haste like Jonah. It is stated:

(4) So wait with patience for the command of thy Lord and be not like companion of the fish when he cried out in agony. Had not Grace from his Lord reached him, he would indeed have been cast of on the naked shore in disgrace. Thus his Lord chose him and made him of the righteous. (lxviii. 48-50)

Jonah was chosen by God's grace and mercy to be His apostle to Nineveh. If in his human frailty he lost a little patience, he suffered for it, but his true and sincere repentance and faith in God's goodness and mercy saved him from his physical and mental distress and from the obscuration of the spiritual light in him.

The lessons from Jonah's story are:

(*i*) That no man should take upon himself to judge of God's wrath or God's mercy.

(*ii*) That God forgives sins on true repentance whether they be in a righteous man or in a wicked people, and

(*iii*) That God's plan will always prevail and can never be defeated.

XI

THE STORY OF THE PROPHET AYYUB
(JOB)

(May peace and blessings of God be on him)

The Qur'an calls the Prophet Job of the Bible as Ayyub and mentions him along with several other prophets in iv. 163 and vi. 85. He is represented as the embodiment of patience and perseverance, and a pattern of humility and faith in God.

(1) And remember Ayyub (Job) when he cried to his Lord: Truly distress has seized me, but Thou art the most Merciful of those that are merciful. So, We listened to him and We removed the distress that was on him and We restored his people and doubled their number as a grace from Ourselves and a thing for commemoration for all who serve Us. (xxi. 83-84).

According to the Book of Job in the Old Testament, Job was a prosperous man, with faith in God, living somewhere in the north-east corner of Arabia. He suffered from a number of calamities. His cattle were destroyed, his servants slain by the sword, and his family crushed under his roof. But he held fast to his faith in God. As a further calamity he was covered with loathsome sores from head to foot. He lost his peace of mind and cursed the day he was born. His false friends came and attributed his afflictions to sin. God recalled to him all His mercies and he resumed his humility and gave up self-justification. He was restored to prosperity with twice as much as he had before. His brethren and friends came back to him. He had a new family and seven sons and three daughters. He lived to a good old age and saw four generations of his descendants.

The Qur'an refers to him in another context thus:

(2) And commemorate Our servant Ayyub. He cried to his Lord: Indeed the Evil one has afflicted me with distress

and suffering. (The command was given:) Strike with the foot; there is water wherein to wash, cool and refreshing, and to drink. And We gave him back his people and doubled their number as a grace from Ourselves and a thing for commemoration for all who have understanding. (And We said to him:) Take in thy hand a little grass and strike therewith and break not (thy oath). Truly We found him full of patience and constancy. How excellent in Our service ever did he turn to Us. (xxxviii. 41-44).

The distress of Ayyub was manifold. But he did not lose faith and always turned to God.

God turned to him with mercy and he was recuperated. He was commanded to strike the earth with his foot and a fountain gushed forth to give him a bath to clean his body from the evil disease, to refresh his spirits, and to give a sustaining drink. This is a touch not mentioned in the Book of Job but adding beautifully to our realisation of the picture.

In his worst distress Job was patient and constant in faith but apparently his wife was not. According to the Book of Job 2: 9-10:

Then said his wife unto him Dost thou still retain thine integrity? curse God, and die. But he said unto her. Thou speakest as one of the foolish women speaketh. What? shall we receive good at the hand of God, and shall we not receive evil? In all this did not Job sin with his lips.

The Qur'an does not give these details but gives a suggestion that he must have said in haste to the woman that he would beat her. He is asked not to correct her with only a wisp of grass to show that he was gentle and humble as well as patient and constant.

The example of Job is given to illustrate that those who lay their faith in the goodness of God under all circumstances and trials of life are never deprived of their reward from God. The Qur'an gives them the assurance that:

(3) Those who, when a misfortune befalls them, say: Surely we are Allah's and to Him shall we surely return. These are those on whom are blessings and mercy from their Lord and those are the followers of the right course. (ii. 156-157).

XII

THE STORY OF THE PROPHET MUSA
(MOSES)

(May peace and blessings of God be on him)

"We recite to the (O Muhammad) from the account of Musa and Fir'aun with truth for a people who believe." (xxviii. 3).

Moses is the most frequently mentioned of all the prophets spoken of in the Qur'an and the details of his life are dwelt upon to a much greater extent than those of any other prophet's life. Why was so much importance given to his history is a point to consider.

In the earlier chapters revealed during the Prophet's stay at Mecca there are only brief references to Moses and the incidents connected with him. The Prophet had to deal here mostly with the idolatrous Quraish of Mecca and, therefore, we find the principles of the faith of Islam discussed in details in these revelations. But when he migrated to Medina he had also to deal with the people of the Book, the Jews and the Christians, living in and around Medina. As far as the principles of religion were concerned, there was very little difference between the teachings of the Qur'an and those of the original Torah and the Evangel. But the people of the Book in general and the Jews in particular were most callous in the observance of these teachings and had tampered with the books. To make them realise their error it was necessary to call to their mind the most important features of their history and to show how far they have strayed away from the path of truth which their scriptures had laid down for them. These were the people receiving the guidance of God ever since the time of Jacob (Israel) through several prophets bringing the guidance of God and prophesying the advent of the last messenger of God and yet these were the very people who greatly misused their privileges and were the most forward of all to reject the last Prophet in spite of a clear prophecy of Moses which says:

> The Lord thy God will raise up unto thee a Prophet from the midst of thee, of thy brethren, like unto me; unto him ye shall hearken,.... I will raise them up a Prophet from among. their brethren, like unto thee, and will put my words in his mouth (Deut. 18: 15-18).

It is to be noted that they are told twice that the promised prophets who shall be like Moses shall appear from among their brethren and we have already pointed out in the story of Abraham that the Arabs are the descendants of Ishmael the one of Abraham and, therefore, they are the brethren of the Israelites. No-Israelite prophet ever claimed to be the like of Moses and even Jesus, the last among the prophets of Israel did never say that he was the like of Moses. Even after the supposed crucifixion of Jesus his disciples awaited the fulfilment of that prophecy. See Acts 3: 22 wherein it is stated:

> For Moses truly said unto the fathers. A Prophet shall the Lord your God raise up unto you of your brethren, like unto me.

The Qur'an, in one of its earliest revelations, points out the fulfilment of this prophecy in these words:

(1) We have sent to you a Messenger, a bearer of witness to you, as We sent a messenger to Fir'aun. (lxxiii. 15).

This claim is made plainer still in a later revelation.

(2) Say what think ye? If it is from Allah and you disbelieve in it, and a witness from among the children of Israel has borne witness of one like him. (xlvi. 10)

In unfolding the history of Moses and his followers, the Jews, the aim of the Qur'an is not only to reclaim the Jews to Islam but at the same time to teach the followers of Muhammad (may peace and blessings of God be on him) that they should avoid all those pitfalls into which the followers of Moses had fallen and also to assure them that after being guided if they behave in the manner of the Jews, eventually their fate will be no better than that of the Jews.

With this object in view the Qur'an has quoted the irrefutable incidents of the life of Moses as evidence of the truth of the claim of the last Prophet, preparing for them a straight path to reach the goal of godliness set for them.

In this context it should be noted that some of the commentators of the Qur'an have included in their commentaries much of the folklore that was prevalent among the Jews, but as these accounts are not based on any authentic source, they cannot be relied upon. We have tried in this chapter to present to our readers a continuous account of the history of Moses which is widely scattered in the pages of the Qur'an.

I. The Tyranny of Pharaoh over the Israelites

(3) Surely Fir'aun[26] exalted himself in the land and divided its people into parties, oppressing one party from among them by killing their sons and sparing their women. Surely he was one of the mischief-makers.
And We desired to bestow a favour upon those who were oppressed in the land and to make them leaders and the heirs and to grant them power in the land to make Fir'aun and Haman[27] and their hosts see from them what they feared. (xxviii. 4-6)

---

26. The word Fir'aun in the Qur'an for Pharaoh in the Bible may look to a superficial observer to be only a difference of pronunciation but this is not so. Pharaoh is undoubtedly the Hebriased title of the King of Egypt. If the Prophet had heard this title from the Jews there was no reason why he should not have used Pharaoh (Fero) in Arabic and its pronunciation was not difficult for the Arabs. But he did not do it and there must be some reason for it. That reason has come to light now from the book of Herodotus, the Greek historian of ancient Greece. He uses Peroun for Pharaoh, the very title the Qur'an has used Herodotus's information must be direct and first-hand. Was this true also of Muhammad? Yes, in one sense, for the real author of the Qur'an is far better informed than the Jews, and if, later, a Greek historian whose work could never have been consulted by the Prophet in Mecca accidentally comes to confirm the Qur'anic name, it should give some food for reflection to those who glibly talk of Muhammad obtaining his information from the Jews or from the folk-lore popular in Arabia in his days.

27. The Christian critics point out that Haman who is mentioned here as the minister of Pharaoh is not mentioned in the Bible as such and therefore, they allege that the Prophet has blundered and confounded the Haman mentioned in the book of Esther of the Old Testament, a favourite of the Persian king Abasuerus with the minister of Pharaoh. But this allegation is based on ignorance combined with prejudice as we shall presently prove.

The two parties were the Israelites and the Egyptians, the latter being the task-masters of the former corresponding to the parties

---

The Pharaoh who was the contemporary of Moses was Rameses II belonging to the nineteenth dynasty of Egypt. During his reign some of the biggest temples and buildings of Egypt were constructed and the head priests of the temples enjoyed great power in the land. Among these the high priest of the temple of Ammon, the Ram-god was the most powerful (*Jewish Encyclopaedia*, Vol. X, p. 12)

Dr. Steindroff of the Leipzig University, in the book *Religious of Ancient Egyptians*, states on page 96 that the high priest of the temple of Ammon was the chief officer in charge of constructions and decorations of all public buildings and he also used to be the general of the military attached to the temples like the archbishops of medieval Europe. He was also in charge of the public treasury and the head of all the priests of the temples of Thebes and of north and the south Egypt, Again on page 106 he writes that the servants of the temples were mostly prisoners of war or the cultivators and artisans of the land. Forced labour was imposed on them all in the construction of public buildings. The priests were very wealthy and exercised great power over the people. The high priest of the. temple of Ammon was owner of one-tenth of the whole of land.

Now keeping these things in view which the European orientalists have discovered from the study of Egyptian archaeology let us see that the Qur'an says about Haman. "Surely Fir'aun and Haman and their hosts were wrong-doers." (xxviii. 8)

No doubt Pharaoh was the king, but the high priest of Ammon with his retinue was also of no less importance and therefore the Qur'an uses the words "and their hosts."

,Again in the same chapter the Qur'an says: "And Fir'aun said: O chiefs I do not know of any god for you besides myself and therefore burn me then, O Haman! bricks of clay and build me a lofty tower that I may mount up to the Lord of Musa, for, in sooth I deem him a liar," (xxviii 38)

This shows that the high priest of Ammon was also the chief architect of the kingdom. Now why did the Qur'an call him Haman? The simple reply is that in the Old Testament the brother of Moses is called Aaron who was the high priest of the Israelites and the Qur'an has called him Harun. Like was the high priest of Ammon is called Haman in place of Ammon.

In the city of Munich in Germany there is an ancient statue on which is written that it is the statue or the high priest of Ammon of the time of Rameses II (*vide* Dr Steindroff, op. cit, pp. 97-98). The Muslim commentators of the Qur'an called Haman as the vizier of Paraoh without

at Mecca, the idolatrous Quraish whowere the oppressors and the
followers of the Prophet who were the oppressed.

Pharaoh and his counsellors, fearing that the Israelites, who
were aliens in the land of Egypt, might one day become powerful
and supreme in the land, oppressed and persecuted them in various
ways.

II. The Childhood of Moses

(4)   And We revealed to Musa's mother saying: Give him suck,
      then when thou fearest for him, cast him into the river
      and do not fear nor grieve; surely We will restore him to
      thee and make him one of the apostles. (xxviii. 7)

In an other place the same incident is expressed in these words:

(5)   Call to mind the occasion when We revealed to thy mother:
      Put him into a chest, then, cast it down into the river,
      then the river shall throw him on the shore, then shall
      take him up one who is an enemy to Me and enemy to
      him and I cast down upon thee love from Me and that
      thou mightest be brought up before My eyes. (xx 38-39).

Moses was born at a time when Pharaoh had commanded all
male children born to the Israelites to be thrown into the Nile.
Moses's mother kept him concealed for three months and at last
unable to hide him any longer threw him into the river in an ark
of bulrushes whence he was picked up by Pharaoh's wife.

(6)   And Fir'aun's followers took him up that he might be an
      enemy and a grief for them, Surely Fir'aun and Haman
      and their hosts were wrong-doers.

---

any proof and the Christian critics of the Qur'an took this opportunity
to level the charge of historical blunder against the Qur'an, but recent
researches have furnished the proofs, See *Encyclopaedia Britannica*, Vol.
IX, 11th edition, p. 54, where it is stated that along with many other
powers the high priest of Ammon used to be appointed as the vizier in
charge of southern Egypt. Indeed what the Qur'an has stated fourteen
hundred years ago is being proved by modern researches day by day
and why should it not be so when the All-Knowing God Himself says;
"This is of the announcements relating to the unseen which We reveal
to thee (O Muhammad)" (cxii 192 and iii, 43), but those blinded with
prejudice can hardly see the truth.

And Fir'aun's wife said: Joy of the eye to me and to thee: do not slay him; may be he will be useful to us or we may take him for a son. But they knew not what they did. And the heart of Musa mother was free from anxiety; she would have almost disclosed it had We not strengthened her heart so that she might be of the believers. And she said to his sister: Follow him up. So she watched him from a distance while they did not perceive.

And We caused him to refuse the nurses his sister came and said: Shall I point to you the people of a house who will take care of him for you and they will be benevolent to him.

So We restored him to his mother that her eyes might be refreshed and that she might not grieve and that she might know that the promise of Allah is true, but most of them do not know. (xxviii. 8-13).

So Moses was brought up in the house of Pharaoh like a prince; a reference of this is given in another place in the Qur'an in these words:

(7) So Pharaoh said: Did we not bring thee up as a child among us for many years of thy life. (xxvi. 18)

III. Moses Kills an Egyptian and is Warned

(8) And when he attained his maturity and became full-grown, We granted him wisdom and knowledge and thus do We reward those who do good.

And he went into the city at a time of unvigilance on the part of its people. He found therein two men fighting, one being of his party and the other of his foes, and he who was of his party cried out to him for help against him who was of the enemies. Moses struck him with his fist and despatched him. He said: This is of the devil's doing; surely he is an open enemy leading astray.

He said: My Lord! Surely I have done harm to myself, so do Thou protect me. So He protected him; Surely He is the Forgiving, the Merciful. He said: My Lord! Because Thou hast bestowed a favour on me I shall never be a backer of the guilty.

And he was in the city fearing, awaiting, when lo! he who

had asked his assistance the day before was crying out to him again for aid. Musa said to him: Thou art plainly a most depraved person. And when he would have laid violent hands on him who was their common foe, he said: O Musa! Dost thou intend to kill me as thou killed a person yesterday. Thou desirest nothing but that thou shouldst be a tyrant in the land and thou desirest not to be of those who act aright.

And a man came running from the remotest part of the city. He said: O Musa! Surely the chiefs are consulting together to slay thee. Therefore begone at once. Surely I counsel thee as a friend.

So forth he went therefrom fearing, looking warily about him and said: My Lord! Deliver me from the unjust people. (xxviii. 14-21)

Moses's slaying the Egyptian was accidental and not intentional, for striking with the fist as ordinary people always do is not sufficient to cause the death of a person. Moses's taking the law into his own hand to punish a guilty man was owing to his being confused at the moment as to the step he should take. So he call it as a devil's doing who misleads men. He therefore, at once realises his mistake and prays for Divine protection.

IV. Flight to Midian and Marriage

(9)   And when the turned his face towards Midian he said: May be my Lord guide me in the right path. And when he came to the water of Midian, he found on it a group of men watering and he found beside them two women keeping back their flocks. He said: What is the matter with you? They said: We cannot water until the shepherds take away their sheep from the water, and our father is a very old man.

So he watered their sheep for them, then went back to the shade and said: My Lord! Surely I stand in need of whatever good Thou mayest send down to me. Then one of the two women came to him walking bashfully. She said: My father invites thee that he may give thee the reward of thy having watered for us. So when he came to him and gave to him the account, he said: Fear not. Thou art secure from the unjust people.

Said one of them: O my father! Employ him, surely the best of those that thou canst employ is the strong man, the faithful one. He said: I desire to marry one of these two daughters of mine to thee on condition that you shouldst serve me for eight years, but if thou complete ten, it will be of thine own free will, and I do not wish to be hard to thee. If Allah please, thou wilt find me one of the good.[28] He said: This shall be an agreement between me and thee: whichever of the two terms I fulfil, there shall be no wrongdoing to me and Allah is a witness of what we say. (xxviii. 22-28)

V. The Call of Moses of Prophethood

(10) So when Musa had filled the term and journeyed with his family, he perceived on the side of the mountain a fire. He said to his family: Wait, I have seen a fire, may be I will bring to you from it some news or a brand or fire,

---

28. Christian critical opinion discovers here another example of how the Qur'an commits mistakes in borrowing from the Bible. It says that the Prophet had in mind a confused idea of Jacob making an agreement with Laban to serve him for seven years as a condition of marrying one of his daughters (Genesis, 29: 18) and he invented the story of Moses's marriage. The slightest similarity in incidents like similarity of names (as we have seen in the case of Haman) gives rise in the minds of the Christian critics to a conclusion of confusion and anachronism where the Qur'an is concerned. But they intentionally forget that the stories given in the Bible of Laban marrying his daughters with Jacob by fraudulent methods and then Jacob's going to the female slaves of both his wives and producing children from them in Genesis, 29 and 30, are daring examples of incident and even loathsome fiction. The Qur'an is far above borrowing such disgusting and abominable tales. We have quoted these passages for our reader's illumination showing the worth of the Bible narratives. According to Rabbinical accounts as given in the *Jewish Encyclopaedia* Moses lived with Jethro for ten years which corroborates the Qur'anic story in substance and there is nothing in the circumstances that he may have served him during that period in consideration for marrying of his daughters. The Qur'an does not state how many daughters the man had. It only speaks of two of them being in charge of their father's flocks Hened the alleged confusion of this story with that of Laban's two daughters is itself due to confusion of the minds of our Christian critics.

so that you may warm yourself.

And when he came to it, a voice was uttered from the right side of the valley in the blessed spot of the bush, saying, O Musa! surely I am Allah, the Lord of the worlds. (xxviii. 29-30)

(11) Surely I am thy Lord: so put of thy shoes, for thou art in the sacred valley which is blessed twice. I have chosen thee: so hearken to what shall be revealed: verily I am Allah, there is no god but I, therefore serve Me and keep up prayers for My remembrance....And what is that in thy right hand, O Musa! He said: This is my staff; I recline on it and I best the leaves with it to make them fall upon my sheep and I have other uses for it. He said: Cast it down, O Musa! So he cast it down, and behold! it was a serpent running. He said: Take hold of it and fear not. We will restore it to its former state; and thrust thy hand into thine armpit: It shall come out white without hurt. That will be another sign--that We may show thee of Our greater signs. (xx. 22-23)

According to xvii. 101, Moses was given altogether nine signs. These signs are mentioned in detail in the following verses:

(12) And certainly We overtook Fir'aun's people with droughts and diminution of fruits that they may be mindful. But when good befell them they said: This is due to us. And when evil afflicted them, they attributed it to the ill-luck of Musa and those with him. Surely their evil fortune is only from Allah but most of them do not know. And they said: whatever sign thou mayest bring to us to charm us with, we will not believe in thee. Therefore We sent upon them widespread death, and the locusts, and the lice, and the frogs, and the blood, clear signs, but they behaved haughtily and they were a guilty people. And when the plague fell upon them they said: O Musa! Pray for us to thy Lord as He has promised with thee. If thou remove the plague from us, we will certainly believe in thee and we will certainly send away with thee the children of Israel. But when We removed the plague from them till a term which they should attain, lo! they broke their promise. (vii. 130-135).

So these nine signs were: (1) the rod, (2) the shining hand, (3) the drought, (4) the loss of fruits, (5) the widespread death, (6) the locusts, (7) the lice, (8) the frogs, and (9) the blood.

VI. Demand for Helper in Aaron

(13) So, these two shall be two arguments from thy Lord to Fir'aun and his chiefs. Surely they are a transgressing people. He said: My Lord; Surely I killed one of them, so I fear lest they slay me. And my brother Harun, he is more eloquent of tongue than I; therefore send him with me as an aider, verifying me. Surely I fear they would reject me. He said: We will strengthen thy arm with thy brother and We will give you both an authority so that they shall not be able to injure you. Go with Our signs, you two, and those who follow you shall be uppermost. (xxviii. 32-35)

(14) He said: O my Lord! Expand my breast for me and make my affair easy to me. And loosen the knot from my tongue that they may understand my world.[29] And give to me an aider from my family, Harun, my brother-strengthen my back by him and associate him with me in my affair, so that we should glorify Thee much and remember Thee aught oft; surely Thou art seeing us. He said: Thou art indeed granted thy petition! O Musa! (xx. 25-36).

VII. Moses Ordered to go to Pharaoh and Demand the Deliverance of the Israelites

(15) And certainly We tried before them the people of Fir'aun. And there came to them a noble apostle saying: Deliver to me the servants of Allah; surely I am a faithful apostle to you. (xliv. 17-18).

(16) And when you Lord called out to Musa saying: Go to the unjust people, the people of Fir'aun: Will they not guard themselves against evil?
He said: O my Lord! Surely I fear they will reject me, and my breast straitens, and my tongue is not eloquent.

---

29. When Moses was a child he burnt his tongue with a live coal. This caused an impediment in his tongue to speak freely. This fact is not mentioned in the Bible but it is given in Midrash Julkut on Ex. c. 166 and also in Shalsheleth Hakabalab, p. 5 b.

Therefore send Thou Harun to help me. And they have a crime against me; therefore I fear they may slay me. He said: By no means, go you both with Our signs, surely We are with you, hearing. Then, come to Fir'aun and say: Surely we are the messengers of the Lord of the worlds. Then send with us the children of Israel. (xxvi. 10-17).

(17) God both to Fir'aun; surely he has become inordinate. Then speak to him a gentle world, haply he may mind or fear. Both said: O our Lord! Surely we fear that he may hasten to do evil to us or that he may become inordinate. He said: Fear not, surely I am with you both. I do hear and see. So go you both to him and say: Surely we are two apostles of the Lord: therefore and the children of Israel with us and do not torment them. Indeed we have brought to thee a message from thy Lord and peace is on him who follows the guidance. Surely it has been revealed to us that the chastisement will surely come upon him who rejects and turns back. (xx. 43-48)

VIII. Discussion with Pharaoh

(18) Fir'aun asked: Who is your Lord, O Musa? He said: Our Lord is He Who gave to everything its creation, then guided it to its goal. He said: Then what is the state of the former generations? He said: The knowledge there of is with my Lord in the book of His decrees. My Lord errs not nor does He forget, Who made the earth for you an expanse, and made for you therein paths and sent down water from the clouds; then thereby We have brought forth pairs of various herbs. Eat and pasture you cattle. Most surely there are signs in this for those endowed with understanding. (xx. 49-54).

(19) Fir'aun asked: Who is then the Lord of the worlds? He said: The Lord of the heavens and the earth and of all that is between them, if you believe it. Said Fir'aun to those around him: Hear you this? Your Lord, said Musa, and the Lord of your sires of old.

In sooth, your apostle whom He hath sent to you, said Fir'aun, is certainly possessed He said: The Lord of the east and the west is He and what is between them, if you

can understand He said: If you take any god beside me
I will surely put thee in prison. Said Musa: What if I show
thee that which shall be proof of my mission? He said:
Forth with it then if thou speakest the truth.

Then threw he down his staff and lo! it was an obvious
serpent. And he drew forth his hand and to! it appeared
white to the beholders.[30] (xxvi. 23-33)

IX. Pharaoh's Enchanters Vanquished

(20) The chiefs at Fir'aun's people said: Most surely this is an
enchanter possessed of knowledge. He intends to turn you
out of your land. Said Fir'aun: What counsel do you then
give? They said: Put him off and his brother and send
collectors into the cities that they bring to thee every
enchanter possessed of knowledge.

And the enchanters came to Fir'aun and said: We must
surely have a reward if we are the prevailing ones. He
said: Yes, and ye shall be certainly of those who are near
to me. They said: O Musa! Will you cast or shall we be
the first to cast? He said: Cast. So when they cast, they
deceived the people's eyes and frightened them and they
produced a mighty enchantment.

And We revealed to Musa saying: Cast thy rod. Then lo!
it devoured their lying wonders. So the truth was made
strong and that which they had wrought proved in vain.
And they were vanquished on the spot and drew back
humiliated. And the enchanters prostrated themselves
adoring. They said: We believe in the Lord of the worlds,

---

30. Here again we have an instance of the correctness of the Qur'anic
statement where it differs with the Bible showing the incompleteness of
the Bible narrative. In the 4th chapter of Exodus it is clearly stated that
two signs were given to Moses, that of his rod turning into a serpent
and that of his hand turning white when put into his bosom And when
we read chapter 7 where the performance of these miracles before Pharaoh
is recorded, we find mention only of the miracle of the rod. It is, however
obvious that Moses must have shown the second sign on the rejection
of the first, for he could not have disobeyed the Divine commandment,
nor was the second miracle given to him in vain.

the Lord of Musa and Harun.[31] Fir'aun said: Do you believe in him before I gave you permission? Surely this is a plot secretly devised in this city that you may turn out of it its people, but you shall know what shall happen. I shall certainly cut off your hands and your feet on opposite sides, then will I crucify you all together. (vii. 109-124)

(21) They said: We do not prefer thee to what has come to us of clear arguments and to Him Who has made us. Therefore decide what thou art going to decide: thou canst decide only about this world's life. Surely we have believed in our Lord that He may pardon us our sins and the sorcery to which thou hast foreed us, for Allah is better and more abiding than thou. Whoever comes to his Lord being guilty, for him is surely hell; he shall not die therein nor shall he live. And whoever comes to Him a believer and he has done good deeds, indeed these it is who shall have the high ranks, the gardens of perpetuity beneath which rivers flow, to abide therein, and this is the reward of him who has purified himself. (xx. 72-76)

X. Pharaoh's Opposition to Moses

(22) When he (Musa) came to them with our signs, lo! they laughed at them. And We did not show them a sign but it was greater than its like and We overtook them with chastisement that they may turn. And they said: O enchanter! Call on thy Lord for our sake and He has made the covenant with thee. We shall surely be the followers of the right way.

---

31. The Bible does not speak of the magicians as believers in the Divine mission of Moses and in the Lord of the worlds Whom he represented. But we have mention of this in the Rabbinical literature according to which some Egyptians accompanied Moses when he departed from Egypt which is corroborated by the Bible narrative: "And a mixed multitude also went up with them" (Exodus 12: 39) "For the Egyptians, when the time fixed for Moses's descent from the mountains had expired came in a body, forty thousand of them accompanied by two Egyptian magicians, Yanos and Yambross the same who imitated Moses in producing the signs and the plagues in Egypt" (*Jewish Encyclopaedia*). This is a proof of the truth of the statement made in the Qur'an and of the incompleteness of the Bible narrative.

But when We removed from them the chastisement, lo!
they broke the pledge. And Fir'aun proclaimed among his
people: O my people: Is not the kingdom of Egypt mine?
And these rivers that flow beneath me, do you not then
see? Nay! I am better than this fellow who is contemptible
and who can hardly speak distinctly. Why have not
bracelets of gold been put upon him or why have there
not come with him angels as companions?

So he incited his people to levity and they obeyed him.
Surely they were a transgressing people. (xiii. 47-54).

(23) And the chief of Fir'aun's people said: Dost thou leave
Musa and his people to make mischief in the land and
to forsake thee and thy gods? He said: We will slay their
sons and spare their women and surely we are masters
over them.

Musa said to his people: Ask help from Allah and be
patient. Surely the land is Allah's. He causes such of His
servants to inherit it as he pleases and the end is for those
who guard against evil.

They said: We have been persecuted before thou came to
us and since thou hast come to us. He said: It may be that
your Lord will destroy your enemy and make you rulers
in the land, then He will see how you act. (vii. 127-129)

(24) And Musa said: O my people! If you believe in Allah, then
rely on Him alone if you submit to Allah. So they said:
On Allah we rely. O Our Lord! Make us not subject to
the presecution of the unjust people. And do Thou deliver
us by Thy mercy from the unbelieving people.

And We revealed to Musa and his brother saying: Take
for your people houses to abide in Egypt and make your
houses places of worship and keep prayer and give good
news to the believers.

And Musa said: Our Lord! Surely Thou hast given to
Fir'aun and his chiefs finery and riches in this world's life,
to this end, our Lord, that they lead people astray from
Thy way? Our Lord! Destroy their riches and harden their
hearts so that they believe not until they see the painful
chastisement.

He said: The prayer of you both has indeed been accepted

Therefore continue in the right was and do not follow the
path of those who do not know. (xx. 84-89)

XI. Moses Commanded to Leave Egypt: Splitting the Sea and Drowning of Pharaoh and His Hosts

(25) And certainly We revealed to Musa saying: Travel by night
with My servants, then make for them a dry path in the
sea, not fearing to be overtaken nor being afraid. (xx. 77)

(26) And We revealed to Musa saying: Go away with My
servants travelling by night. Surely you will be pursued,
So Fir'aun sent heralds into the cities. These Israelites, said
they, are a scanty band and yet they have enraged us and
most surely we are numerous and wary.

Thus we caused them to quite of gardens and springs and
treasures and goodly dwellings. Even so, and We gave
them as a heritage to the children of Israel. Then the
Egyptians pursued them at sunrise. So when the two hosts
saw each other the companions of Musa cried out: Most
surely we are being overtaken. He said: By no means.
Surely my Lord is with Me. He will show me a way out.
And We revealed this order to Musa: Strike the sea with
thy rod. And it clove as under and each part became like
a large mountain. Then made We the others draw on and
We saved Musa and those who were with him all, but
We drowned the others. (xxvi. 52-66)

(27) And We made the children of Israel to pass through the
sea, then Fir'aun and his hosts followed them in hostility
and for oppression until, when drowning overtook him,
he said: I believe that there is no god but He in whom
the children of Israel believe and I am of those who submit.
What now! said God, and indeed thou has been rebellious
hitherto and wast of the mischief-makers. But this day We
save thee in thy body[32] that thou mayest be a sign to those

---

32. The Bible does not mention that the body of Pharaoh was cast
ashore. But from recent discoveries in Egyptology it has been found that
the body of Rameses II who is regarded as the Pharaoh of Moses's time
has been preserved among the mummies of Egypt (*vide Encyclopaedia
Britannica*, Article: 'Mummy"). This is another instance of the insufficiency

after thee and most surely most people are heedless of Our signs. (xx. 90-92).

XII. Moses Receives the Law

(28) And We appointed with Musa a time of thirty nights and completed them with ten more. So the appointed time of his Lord was complete forty nights. And Musa said to his brother Harun: Take my place among my people and act will and do not follow the way of the mischief-makers. And when Musa came at Our appointed time and his Lord spoke to him, he said: My Lord! Show me Thyself, so that I may look upon Thee. He said: Thou canst not bear to see Me. But look at the mountain, if it remains firm in its place, than will thou see Me. But when his Lord manifested His glory to the mountain, He made it crumble and Musa fell down in swoon. Then, when he recovered he said: Glory be to Thee: I turn to Thee and I am the first of believers.

He said: O Musa! Surely I have chosen thee above the people with My messages and with My words; therefore, take hold of what I give to thee and be of the grateful ones. And We ordained for him in the tablets admonition of every kind and clear explanation of all things. Take hold of them with firmness and enjoin the people to take hold of what is best thereof.[33] (vii. 142-145)

---

of the Bible narrative and the truth of the Qur'anic statement where it supplements the Bible. Surely the discovery now made could not have been known to the Holy Prophet and here we have a clear example of the superhuman knowledge contained in the Qur'an. The contention of the Christian critics that the stories of the Qur'an are borrowed from the Bible falls flat to the ground.

33. According to the Bible, Moses received the Torah in the form of tablets written by the hand of God "The tablets were the work of God and the writing was writing of God graven upon the tablets. (Exodus, 32: 16). But according to the Qur'an the Torah was revealed to Moses in the same manner as books were revealed to other prophets and as the Qur'an was revealed to the Prophet of Islam. "Who revealed the Book which Muta brought?" (vi 92); 'We have sent revelations to thee as We sent revelations to Nuh and prophets after him" (vi. 163)

XIII. Israelites Worship the Calf

(29) And Musa people made of their ornaments a calf after him, a mere body which had a hollow sound. What! Could they not see that it did not speak to them nor guide them in the way? They took it for worship and they were unjust. And when they repented and saw that they had gone astray they said: If our Lord show not mercy to us, we shall certainly be of the losers.

And when Musa returned to his people wrathful and in violent grief, he said: Evil is it that you have done after me. Did you turn away from the bidding of your Lord. And he threw down the tablets[34] and seized his brother by the head dragging him towards him. He said: Son of my mother, surely the people reckoned me weak and had wellnigh slain me, therefore make not the enemies rejoice over me and count me not among the unjust people.[35]

---

34. According to the Bible, Moses in his anger broke the tablets on which the word of God was written (Ex 32: 19) and Ex. 34: 1 describes how they were renewed, but the Qur'an says that he only put them down and took them up again when his anger calmed. It appears strange indeed that a prophet like Moses should have been so overpowered with wrath as to have broken the tablets upon which were written down Divine communications. Therefore the Bible narratives must be rejected. Its absurdity is to be found in the fact that the tablets of stone written with the finger of God by merely being cast out of his hand, as the Bible says, had been so broken as to make the writing illegible. Therefore the Qur'anic statement which contradicts the Bible is the correct one.

35. In chapter 32 of Exodus the people cause Aaron to make a calf out of their golden ornaments. He fashions the calf with graving tool after melting the gold into the shape of a calf and builds an altar for it and offers burnt offerings. God informs Moses of their transgression and whishes to destroy them all. Moses beseaches the Lord not to be angry and reminds Him of the promise He gave to Abraham, Isaac and Israel and God repents for the evil which He thought to do to the Israelites. Imagine the enormity of accusing God of committing an evil and repenting for it. Moses returns to his people, casts the tablets out of his hand and breaks them beneath the mount and takes Aaron to task for the sin he committed. Aaron confesses his fault and the chapter ends with the words: "And the Lord paluged the people because they made the calf which Aaron made." The Qur'an not only clears him of idol-making but shows

He said: My Lord! Forgive me and my brother and cause us to enter into Thy mercy, for Thou art the Most Merciful of the merciful ones. (vii. 148-151)

This incident of the worship of the calf is described in another context by the Qur'an thus:

(30) He said: We have tried thy people after thee and the Samiri[36] has led them astray.

---

him as plainly warning the Israelites because of the worship of the calf in these words: "O my people, you are only tried by it and surely your Lord is the Beneficent God; therefore follow me and obey my orders." (xx. 90)

Here Aaron's excuse and Moses's acceptance of it show clearly that Aaron was quite innocent, having had a share neither in making the calf nor in worshipping it. The Bible account which makes a righteous prophet of God guilty of the most heinous crime must be rejected as untrue. Here is another example of the Qur'an championing the cause of the prophets of God and clearing them of the blasphemies that the compilers of the Bible have heaped upon their sacred memories.

36. Who was this Samiri? As the Bible does not mention the name of any such person, the adverse Christian critics of the Qur'an at once jump to the conclusion that the Qur'an has committed a blunder of anachronism. According to these critics, the Jewish capital Samarjah was founded about 925 B.C. long after the Exodus and a tribe by The name of Samaritans sprang up from this place which was a cross-breed of the Israelites and the Gentiles, and calf worship was in vogue among these people. *Perhaps* Muhammad learnt this from the Jews at Mecca and fabricated this story in connection with Moses. We have seen under footnote 2 how in the case of Haman, the high pries of Ammon, they made similar accusations and how the truth of the Qur'an was vindicated by the researches in Egyptology. A similarity in names becomes enough authority with these oriental scholars where Muhammad or the Qur'an is concerned and that is enough excuse to accuse the Qur'an or the Prophet.

There is every possibility of this Samiri to be some ancestor of the Samaritans. What the Qur'an says in this verse is that some person other than Aaron was responsible for making the calf From Rabbinical literature (see *Jewish Encyc.*, Art: "Calf") it appears that the Egyptians who had come with the Israelites were foremost in demanding the making of the calf. Imam Razi in his commentary asserts that he was an Egyptian who had believed in Moses and come along with the Israelites.

So, Musa returned to his people wrathful and sorrowing. Said he: O my people! Did not your Lord promise you a goodly promise; did then the time seem long to you of my absence or desired ye that wrath from your Lord should light upon you that ye failed in your promise to me? They said: We did not break our promise to thee of our own accord but we were made to bear the burden of the ornaments of the people, then we cast them away. Thus did Samiri suggest to us.

So he brought forth for them a calf, a mere body which had a hollow sound and they said: This is your God and the God of Musa whom he hath forgotten.

What! Could they not see that it did not return to them a reply and that it did not control any harm or benefit for them. And Harun certainly had said to them before: O my people! You are only tried by it and surely your Lord is the Beneficient God; therefore follow me and obey my orders.

They said: We will by no means cease to keep to it worship until Musa returns to us.

Musa said: O Harun! What prevented thee when thou sawest them go astray from following me? Hast thou then disobeyed me commands? He said: O son of my mother! Seize me not by my beard nor by my head. Surely I was afraid lest thou shouldst say: Thou hast caused a division among the children of Israel and not waited for my word. He said: What was then thy object, O Samiri? He said: I saw what they did not see. So I followed only partly the way of the apostle, then I cast it away; thus did my soul embellish to me. He said: Begone, then, surely for thee it will be in this life to say, touch me not, and surely there is a threat for thee which thou shalt not escape. Look at thy god to whose worship thou didst keep so long. We will certainly burn it, then we will certainly scatter it a wide scattering in the sea.[37] You God is only Allah; there

---

37. This shows that the ashes of the calf were thrown into the sea and the story of the Israelites being made to drink water mixed with the ahses of the calf is not credited by the Qur'an as given in Exodus, 32:

is no god but He and He comprehends all things in His knowledge. (xx. 85-98)

XIV. Order to Slaughter a Cow

The idea of calf or bull-worship seems to have been taken from the Egyptians. In the opinion of Renan, Maspers, and Konig, "Bull-worship may have been an imitation of the worship of Apis at Memphis or Mendes at Heliopolis." (*Encyclopaedia Biblica*, col. 631)

The writer of the article on the golden calf is, however, of opinion-that "Adoption from Egypt is unlikely," and his chief reason is that "the Egyptians worshipped only living animals." But the Israelites too seemed to have been addicted to the worship of living animals in the time of Moses as the incident given below shows and the calf was only an image of the living animal. At any rate, four hundred years of contact with the Egyptians could not have been without its influence, a bull worship dating from a very remote antiquity in Egypt must have had some effect. It was for this reason that the Mosaic law laid great stress on the slaughter of cows and the commandment mentioned below seems to have been given for the same reason. Notwithstanding all that Moses did to uproot this form of idolatry from among the Israelites, the worshipping of the bull appears to have continued up to the

---

20, and Deut. 2: 21. The ring-leaders among the Israelites show seduced the people to calf-worship were slain by the Levites. The Bible states that three thousand people were killed on that day. Therefore there was no need of making them drink the water containing the ashes of the calf.

The Qur'an, on the other hand, tells us: "And when Musa said to his people: O my people! you have surely been unjust to yourselves by taking the calf for a god. Therefore turn to you Creator penitently and mortify yourselves. That is best for you with your Creator. So He turned to you mercifully, for surely He is the oft-returning to mercy, the Merciful," (ii. 54). Thus the wrong was forgiven, though it is possible that the forgiveness may have been granted after the sentence was executed. It is however strange that Aaron, who according to the Bible, made the image and led the people to calf-worship was not at all punished. This itself is enough to show that the allegation made against him in the Bible was baseless.

time of Hosea who rails at it in very strong terms. (*vide Hosea*,
8: 5 and 10: 5)

> (31) When Musa said to his people: Surely Allah commands
> you that you should sacrifice a cow.[38]
> They said: Dost thou ridicule us? He said: I seek the
> protection of Allah from being one of the ignorant. They
> said: Call on thy Lord for our sake to make it plain to us
> what she is. Musa said: He says, surely she is a cow neither
> advanced in age nor too young, or middle age between
> that and this. Do therefore what you are commanded. They
> said: Call on thy Lord forour sake to make it plain to us
> what her colour is. Musa said: He says, she is a yellow
> cow, her colour is intensely yellow, giving delight to the
> beholders. They said: Call on thy Lord for our sake to make
> it plain to us what she is, for, surely to us the cows are
> all alike and if Allah please, we shall surely be guided
> aright. Musa said: He says, surely she is a cow not made
> submissive to plough the land nor does she irrigate the

---

38. The slaughter of a cow referred to in this verse has nothing in
common with the slaying of the heifer as an expiation of the uncertain
murder in Deut. 21: 1-9 or to the slaughter of a red heifer, the ashes
of which purify one who was touched the dead body of any man (Num.
19: 1-9) except the fact that as the Israelites held the cow in great honour
and even worshipped it, as is clear from their worship of the golden calf,
they were ordered to slaughter such cows as were usually let abroad and
worshipped as sacred objects-cows not wrought with nor drawn in yoke
but let loose to wander abroad and the cow mentioned in these verses
is a typical cow answering this description. This type of cow is still an
object of special reverence in India. The slaughter of this particular type
was specially enjoined upon the Jews according to the Bible as well as
the Holy Qur'an the object being to root out cow-worship among them,
But whereas the Biblical injunction to slaughter a heifer is a general
injuction to be observed whenever an uncertain murder takes place or
an unclear person is to be purified the injunction as contained in the
Qur'an points to the slaughter of one particular cow which was probably
likely to become an object of worship. Indeed there is a striking
resemblance between the colour of the golden calf and the cow ordered
to be slaughtered. The concluding words of the passage show that because
of their reverence for that particular cow, the Jews were very averse to
slaughter it. This incident is entirely ignored by the Bible.

tilth, sound, without a blemish in her. They said: Now you have brought the truth. So they sacrificed her though they had not the mind to do it. (ii. 67-71)

XV Divine Favours on Israelites and their Stubbornness

(32) We made the clouds to give shade over you and We sent to you Manna and Salwa. Eat of the good things that We have given you. (ii. 57)

(33) And when Musa prayed for drink for his people, We said: Strike the rock with thy rod and from it there gushed twelve fountains, each tribe knew their drinking place. Eat and drink, said We, of what God hath supplied and do no wrong on the earth by licentious deeds. (ii. 60)

(34) And (remember) when ye said: O Musa! we will not put up with one sort of food; pray therefore to thy Lord for us that He may bring forth for us of that which the earth groweth, its herbs, and its cucumbers and its garlic and its lentils and its onions. He said: what! will you exchange that which is worse for what is better? Then enter a city that you may have what you ask for. (ii 61).

(35) And We made a covenant with you under the lofty mountain heights and (said): Take hold of what We have given you with firmness and bear in mind what is in it, so that you become righteous, you turned back after that. Were it not for the grace of Allah and His mercy on you, you would certainly have been losers: (ii. 63-64)

(36) And when Musa said to his people: O my people! Remember the favour of Allah upon you when He raised prophets among you, and made you kings and gave you what He had not given to any among the nations. O my people! enter the holy land which Allah has prescribed for you and turn not on your backs, for then, you will turn back losers.

They said: O Musa! surely there is a strong race in it, and we will on no account enter it until they go out from it: so, if they go out from it, then, surely we will enter...Go therefore thou and thy Lord, then fight you both; surely we will here sit down. He said: My Lord! I have no control upon any but my own self and my brother; therefore make a separation between us and the transgressing people. He said: So it shall surely be forbidden to them for forty years, they shall wander about in the land; therefore do not grieve for the transgressing people. (v. 20-26)

XVI. Mose's Own People Make False Imputations Against Him.

(37) O you who believe! Be not like those who spoke evil things of Musa but Allah cleared him of what they said and he was worthy of regard with Allah.[39] (xxxiii. 69)

(38) And when Musa said to his people: O my people! Why do you cause me grief when you know that I am Allah's apostle to you. But when they turned aside, Allah made the hearts turn aside and Allah doth not guide the transgressing people. (lxi. 5)

XVII. Lessons from the Story of Moses

The importance attached to the life-story of Moses in the Qur'an is due to the fact of his likeness with the Holy Prophet Muhammad (may peace and the blessings of Allah be upon him). Moses was both a law-giver and a nation-builder and so was the Holy Prophet. The Israelites had been in a state of slavery to the Pharaoh of Egypt

---

39. The Bible has ascribed a very despicable act of Moses. In the book of Numbers, chapters 12, verse I, it is written that the sister of Moses, Miryam, charged him with illicit connection with a Cushite woman and the God of Moses became angry with her and made her leper but on the prayer of Moses she was restored again to health. The Qur'an rejects this story in the verses quoted above.

Further on, the Bible paints Moses as a heartless tyrant inflicting vengeance on the Midianites for the doubtful fault of one Midianite woman who was supposed to beguile an Israelite. In retribution he wages war against the midanites in which all the males are slain and all the women and children are taken captive and all their flocks and herds and goods are taken and all their cities and castles are burnt. When the spoils of this war are taken to Moses he gets angry with his men for having spared the women and children and he orders to kill every woman that hath known man by lying with him, in cold blood and distributes the virgins and the little ones among his followers to be their slaves and those numbered thirty-two thousand souls in all, (*vide* chapter 31, Numbers).

for about four centuries. It was, therefore, a hard task for Moses to build a nation out of them but this task was very limited in comparison to the work with which the Holy Prophet was entrusted. He had to build a nation on quite a new principle, a nation, not united by any ties of blood, race, colour or county but united by a moral and spiritual outlook, united by a belief in the Unity of God and His all-pervading Lordship. Such was to be the Muslim nation in which the Arab and the non-Arab, the white and the black, the Semitic and the Aryan, were all to be on one level. The whole world was the country and the whole humanity the race out of which this nation was to be formed. With this apparently impossible task, the Prophet was entrusted; and single-handed in the face of all difficulties he built up the foundation of a new nation within a short period of twenty-three years. An accomplishment like this cannot be placed to the credit of any other man in the history of the world.

As both Moses and Muhammad were nation-builders and lawgivers, many were the occasions in the life of the former that resembled those which faced the latter and therefore these are recalled to show that what happened to the opponents of Moses was sure to happen to those who now opposed the Prophet and the same God who delivered Moses and his people from the bondage of the Pharaohs is at the back of the Prophet and He is powerful enough to change the situation in his favour by means unperceived by human mind. Whatever respite is being given by God to a people to reform themselves, if not utilised in time, for their own betterment, will not be prolonged, and repentance will do them no good when the chastisement is in sight, as was the case with the Pharaoh at the moment of his drowning. The followers of the Prophet should not despair of the mercy of God if success is delayed in their affairs, for, it is the righteous only that ultimately win. They should also bear in mind that when they are delivered of their enemies, they should not tread the path of the Israelites which they adopted after their liberation from the slavery of the Egyptians. Take for instance their behaviour, when they were ordered to slaughter a cow. Here is a lesson for the Muslims that in carrying out the Divine injunctions they should not seek the refuge of lame excuses but obey the behests under all circumstances with the spirit of ready compliance and with a willing heart. The principle laid down for them is expressed in two meaningful words: *Sama'na wa Ata'na*, i.e., we have heard and we obey.

In the course of the history of Moses the Qur'an has pointed out the main traits of the character of the Israelites with the object of warning the Muslims lest they take to a similar path and meet the same fate which the Israelites had come to. Let us briefly note what the Qur'an has said about them.

(1) *Sectarianism.* The People of the Book were divided into many sects and each sect was condemning the other out of their mutual jealousies, even though they possessed the same scriptures. The Qur'an warns the Muslims in these words:

> (39) Surely they who divided their religion into parts and became sects, you have no concern with them. (vi. 160)

Again:

> (40) Be not of those who divide their religion and became parties, every sect rejoining in what they have with them. (xxx. 32)

Or:

> (41) Hold fast by the cable of Allah all together and be not disunited. (iii. 102)

And also:

> (42) Allah revealed the Book with truth and those who differed in the Book have drifted away from it. (ii. 176)

(2) *Interpolations in Divine Scriptures.* They used to make changes to suit their whims and fancies. The Qur'an points out their mischievous dealings in these words:

> (43) Those who were unjust changed the word into other than what was given them. (ii. 59)

Or:

> (44) Woe to those who transcribe the Book corruptly with their hands and say it is from God in order that they may sell it for some price. Woe then to them for the gains they have made thereby. (ii. 79)

Again it is said:

> (45) There is a party of them who used to listen to the word of God and yet knowingly perverted it and they knew what they were doing. (ii. 81)

(3) *Suppression of Truth.* They used to hide the truth that was

revealed in their scriptures. The Qur'an points it out in these words:

(46) Clothe not what is true with what is untrue or knowingly suppress the truth. (ii. 142)

They were expecting the advent of a prophet according to prophecies contained in their scriptures, but when the same prophet did appear, they did not leave any stone unturned to destroy him for the simple reason that he belonged to the Ishmaelites instead of the Israelites. The Qur'an points this out in these words:

(47) And believe in what I have sent down confirming that which is already with you and do not take the lead in rejecting it. (ii. 41)

and when any one of them would recite any portion of their scripture before the Muslims which supported the claim of the Prophet they used to say:

(48) Blab ye to them what Allah has disclosed to you that they may throw it back at you as the very thing received from your Allah. Can you not understand this much? (ii. 76)

In spite of their knowing full well that the Prophet was the promised Messiah of their scriptures they would not recognise him. This is pointed out in the Qur'an in these words:

(49) Those whom We have given the Book recognise him as they recognise their own sons. (ii. 146)

(4) *Fondness of Worldly Gains and Abhorrance of Death.* The Jews were notorious for their fondness of material gains and abhorrance of death which brought upon them disgrace from all quarters. The Qur'an makes mention of this in these words:

(50) And thou wouldst surely find them of all men the most covetous of life, even more covetous than those who associate others with God. Everyone of them may wish to live a thousand years. (ii. 96)

(5) *Selfish Rabbies and Doctors of Law.* The Israelite docros of law had for their own selfish gains usurped the place of God and were obeyed and followed implicitly by their people against the injunctions of their scriptures. The Qur'an points out this weakness of theirs in these words:

(51) They have taken their doctors of law and their priests for lords besides God. (ix. 31)

They had forgotten their own responsibilities and lived for their

own selfish ends, and their ignorant followers relied implicity on
their exposition of their religious responsibilities.

> (52) Why do their learned men and the doctors of law not
> prohibit them from their speaking of what is sinful and
> their eating of unlawfully acquired things. Certainly evil
> be that which they do. (v. 83)

Their story does not end with this but they had totally neglected
to forbid evil and were obsessed in promoting their own selfish
interests and, if, on any occasion they had any impulse to admonish
others, they would do so forgetting to set themselves aright. The
Qur'an asks them:

> (53) Will you enjoin righteousness on others and neglect to
> practise the same yourselves and yet you profess to follow
> the Book. (ii. 44).

(6) *Indifference Towards the Law.* In every affair of theirs whether
it be temporal or spiritual, the rule of the devil was the order of
the day. Even the few injunctions which had escaped their
interference were only given lip profession and were never put into
practice. They were no doubt bearers of the Torah but no corner
of their life's activities was illuminated with its light. The Qur'an
refers to this in these words:

> (54) The likeness of those who were charged with the Torah
> then did not observe it is the likeness of an ass bearing
> a load of books. (lxii. 5)

They threw aside the Book of God and thereby invoked the curse
of God. To them the Qur'an says:

> (55) Say (to them O Prophet): O people of the Book! you follow
> no good till you keep up the Torah and the Gospel and
> that which is revealed to thee from thy Lord. (v. 68)

(7) *Mutual Enmities.* The Qur'an says that on account of
interpolations in the word of God and breaking the covenants and
neglecting the law, they are made to suffer the curse of mutual
enmities. It says:

> (56) On account of breaking the covenant We cursed them and
> made their hearts hard; they altered the words from their
> places and they neglected a portion of what they were
> reminded of and thou shalt always discover treachery in
> them excepting a few of them and with those who say
> we are Christians, We made a covenant but they neglected

a portion of what they were reminded of; therefore We excited among them enmity and hatred to the day of resurrection. (v. 13-14)

(8) *Devouring the Unlawful.* Love of wealth is the proverbial weakness of a Jew. Even Shakespeare had to expose this their weakness in the notorious character of Shylock. The Qur'an throws light upon this trait of their character in these words:

(57) They are listeners of lies and devourers of what is forbidden. (v. 42)

Or:

(58) Ye who believe! Most surely many of the doctors of law and the monks eat away the property of men falsely and turn them from Allah's way. (ix. 34)

(9) *Cooperation with the Unbelievers and idol-worshippers.* When the Jews, forsaking the path of God, formed themselves into different schisms and when after materialistic attainments, their standard of antagonism eventually underwent a change. On the one hand they claimed to be the chosen people of God and on the other they made friends with the enemies of God and the enemies of the believers. The Qur'an has pointed out their double-sideness in these words;

(59) Thou wilt see many of them befriending those who disbelieve. (v. 80)

When the mind is darkened by animal passions, one loses the talent of distinguishing good from evil. The Qur'an declares in this connection that:

(60) Thou shalt not find a people who believe in Allah and the latter day be friending those who act in opposition to Allah and His apostle even though they were their own fathers or their sons or their brothers or their kinsfolk. (lviii. 22)

But the Jews who professed to believe in God and the Hereafter were foremost in making alliances with the polytheists against the Muslims.

(10) *Seeking Pretexts.* When man gets overpowered with the influx of passions and loses the fear of God, he sacrifices the injunctions of God on the altar of his worldliness. He beings to seek pretexts to avoid correct performance of his duties forgetting that there is an omnipresent and omniscient God who knows the secrets of his heart. The Sabbath day was declared by the law of

Moses as a sacred day and the Jews were forbidden to work for
their livelihood on that day. But their covetous and greedy
temperament could not keep them at home. They transgressed the
law under various pretexts to hoodwink God Himself.[40] The Qur'an
refers to it in these words:

> (61) And certainly you have known those among you who
> exceeded the limits of the Sabbah. We said to them: Be
> as apes despised and hated. (ii. 65)

(11) *Ignorance of the Law and Persistence in Ignorance.* It has been
the rule with the old nations of the world that after the passing
away of their prophets they gradually let the law enforced by them
fall into desuetude and followed self invented rituals and customs
according to their wishes in place of the simple and clear teachings
of their faith. The Israelites were no exception. Thought they had
the Torah with them thought not in its original purity, yet their
religious life was based upon certain superstitious rites and
customs. The Qur'an points this out in these words:

> (62) And there are among them illiterates who know not the
> Book but only idle stories and they only make use of
> conjectures. (ii. 78)

The Qur'an condemns them in these words:

> (63) O people of the Book! Be not unduly immoderate in your

---

40. This was not mentioned in the story of Moses as this incident
did not take place during the life-time of Moses. We read in Ezek, 22:
8-15 the following; "Thou hast despised mine holy things, and has
profaned my Sabbaths. In thee are men that carry tales to shed blood:
and in thee they eat upon the mountains: in the midst of thee they commit
lewdness. In thee have they discovered their fathers' nakedness; in thee
they humbled her that was set apart for pollution. And one hath
committed abomination with his neighbour's wife; and another hath
lewdly defiled his daughter in law; and another in thee hath humbled
his sister, his father's daughter... and I will scatter thee among the
heathen, and disperse thee in countries." All this description conforms
to the character of apes which the Qur'an uses. Moses's prophecy of the
fact of the Jewish nation amply bears out the description as given in the
Qur'an. "And the Lord shall scatter thee among all people, from the one
end of the earth even unto the other....And among these nations shalt
thou find no ease, neither shall the sole of thy foot have rest; but the
Lord shall thee a trembling heart, and falling of eyes, and sorrow of Mind"
(Deut. 28: 64-65)

religion and not follow the low desires of people who went astray before and led many astray and drifted away from the right path. (v. 77)

This is only a birds-eye-view of the state of society among the people of the Book during the Prophetic mission of Muhammad (may peace and the blessings of God be upon him). This picture is drawn in the sacred book of Islam with the object of warning the Muslims that God's law of Requital is universal and undiscriminating and is applied to all without the least distinction of race and creed. For is it not said in the Qur'an.

(64) Thou shalt not find any change in the course of Allah. (xxxiii. 62)

(65) Thou shalt not find any alteration in the course of Allah. (xxxv. 43)

XIII

THE STORY OF THE PROPHET HARUN (AARON)

(May peace and blessings of God be on him)

Harun (Aaron of the Bible) is generally mentioned along with Moses in the Qur'an. He was the elder brother of Moses and on the request of Moses, God blessed him with the gift of Prophethood and made him a messenger unto Pharaoh. This prayer of Moses is described in the Qur'an in these words:

(1) And give to me an aider from my family, Harun, my brother. Strengthen my back by him and associate him with me in my affair, so that we may glorify Thee much and remember Thee oft. Surely Thou art seeing us.

He said: Thou art indeed granted thy petition O Musa (xx. 29-30)

(2) And my brother Harun, he is more eloquent of tongue than I; therefore send him with me as aider, verifying me; surely I fear that they would reject me.

He said: We will strengthen thy arm with thy brother and We will give you both an authority, so that they shall not be able to injure you. Go with Our signs, you two, and those who follow you shall be uppermost.

(3) And certainly We conferred a favour on Musa and Harun and We delivered them both and their people from the mighty distress and We helped them, so they were the vanquishers. As We gave them both the Book that made things clear and We guided them both on the right way and We perpetuated praise to them among the later generations. Peace be on Musa and Harun. Even thus do We reward the doers of good. Surely they were both Our believing servants. (xxxvii. 114-122)

According to the above verse, not only Moses was given the

Book but Harun also was given the Book like all other prophets. The same is stated in another verse thus:

(4) And certainly We gave to Musa and Aaron the Distinction, and a Light and a Reminder for those who would guard against evil. (xxi. 48)

It is generally understood that Torah or Taurat is the specific name of the Book given to Moses but nowhere in the Qur'an is it said that Moses was given Torath or that the Book that was given to Moses was Torah. The Qur'an, no doubt, mentions in several places that Moses was given a book. It is called "Ayat" (i.e., signs) in some places (*vide* vii. 103; x. 75; xxiii. 45) and "Furqan" (i.e., Distinction) in one place (xxi. 48) and "Kitab" (i.e., the Book) in several places (*vide* ii. 87; vi. 92, 155; xi. 110; xvii. 2; xxiii. 49; xxv. 35; xxviii. 43; xxxii. 23; xxxvii 17; xl. 53; xli. 53; xli. 45; xl. 12; etc. and "Suhaf" (i.e., Scriptures) in two places in liii. 36 and lxxxvii. 19 but nowhere does it mention the name Taurat as the name of the book given to Moses. Of course the word Taurat has occurred in several places in the Qur'an but nowhere it is called the book of Moses So, it is not correct to say that the book given to Moses is called Taurat.

The Old Testament also is not the Taulat of the Qur'an. The Old Testament is a Christian term applied to a body of old Jewish records in contradistinction to the New Testament, and there is a difference of opinion between the Roman Catholics and the Protestants as to the number of books to be included in it. For further information on the books of the Old Testament we refer the reader to our essay on "The story of the Bible" in our book *Tenets of Islam.*

The Jews divided their scripture into three parts: (1) The Law, (2) The Prophets, (3) The Writings. The division was probably current during the time of Jesus, for, Jesus, according to the Bible, refers to the Jewish Scriptures in these terms only, viz., the Law, the Prophets and the Psalms (*vide* Luke, 24: 44 and Matt 7: 12). In the Old Testament book II Chronicles 34: 30, the reference to the book of the Covenant must be to the original Law.

The Jews in the Prophets time (and since) went a great deal by the Talmud or a body of oral expositions reduced to writing in different schools of doctors and learned men. The Talmudist in the sixth century of the Christian era before the preaching of Islam, evolved the Massorah, a body of authoritative Jewish Hadith to which references are to be found in passages addressed to the Jews in the Qur'an. What passed as the Taurat or the Law with the Jews in the Prophet's time was the mass 'of these traditional writings and their translations in the Aramic language.

Harun is mentioned in the Qur'an as a prophet along with several other prophets in the following verses: vi. 85; x. 75; xix. 53; xxiii. 45; xxv. 35, 36.

In the story of Moses we have already shown how the Bible attributes the making of the calf to Aaron and how the Qur'an declares Harun innocent in this matter. According to the Bible, the children of Levi were commanded to slay those who took part in the calf-worship and three thousand men were killed on that day but the fact that Harun who is alleged to have made the calf and led the people to calf-worship was left unpunished, is proof enough to show that the charge made against him was false.

In is indeed enigmatic to understand the Jewish mentality how it identifies recognised men of God with idolatry and crimes like incest, fraud, cruelty and treachery, instances of which we have quoted in the foregoing pages.

XIV

THE STORY OF THE PROPHET DAU'D (DAVID)

(May Peace and blessings of God be on him)

David was not only a prophet of the Israelites but he was also their king. He did not inherit any kingdom from his ancestors who were only very common people but he came into prominence after his fight with Goliath. The story given in the Bible can be summed up thus:

David was a raw youth with no arms or armour. He was not known even in the Israelites camp and the Giant Goliath mocked him. Even David's own elder brother chided him for deserting sheep, for, he was a poor shepherd lad to out ward appearance, but his faith had made him more than a match to the Philistine hosts. When Saul offered his own armour and arms to David, the young hero declined to use them as he had not tried them, while his shepherd's sling and staff were his well-tried weapons. He picked up five smooth pebbles on the spot from stream and used his sling to such effect that he knocked down Goliath. He then used Goliath's own sword to slay him. There was consternation in the Philistine army; they broke and fled and were pursued and cut to pieces. Then Saul married his daughter to David and after many an exploit David finally became the king of Israelites.

The whole story is compressed into a few words by the Qur'an from the point of view of narration but its spiritual lessons are dwelt upon from many points of view. The Bible is mainly interested in the narrative which is full of boring details but says little about the universal truths of which every true story is only a parable. The Qur'an assumes the story but tells the parable.

Mark how the Qur'an tells it:

(1) He (Talut, i.e., Saul) and the faithful ones with him said: This day we cannot cope with Jalut (Goliath) and his forces.

But those who were convinced that they would meet their God said: How oft by God's will hath a small force vanquished a big one? God is with those who steadfastly persevere.

When they advanced to meet Jalut and his forces they prayed: Our Lord! Pour out constancy on us and make our steps firm and help us against those who are disbelievers. By God's will they routed them and Da'ud slew Jalut and God gave him power and wisdom and taught him whatever else He willed. (ii. 249-250)

Apart from the main lesson that if we would preserve our national existence and our faith, it is our duty to fight with courage and firmness, there are other lessons in David's story: (1) Numbers do not count but faith, determination and the blessings of God; (2) size and strength are of no avail against truth, courage, and careful planning; (3) the hero tries his own weapons which are available to him at the time and place even though people may laugh at him; (4) if God is with us, the enemy's weapon may become an instrument of his won destruction; (5) personality conquers all dangers and puts heart into our wavering friends; (6) pure faith brings God's reward which may take many forms; in David's case it was power, wisdom, and other gifts, for, he was not only a shepherd, a warrior, king, a wise man, a prophet but was also endowed with the gifts of poetry and music. His Psalms (Zabur) are still extant.

In verse 163* of Surah iv. along with the gifts to several other prophets this special gift that was given by God to David is mentioned in the Qur'an thus:

(2) And We gave to Da'ud Zabur. (iv. 163)

All the English translators of the Qur'an have translated the word "Zabur" by the words Psalms of David found in the Old Testament. These Psalms are now considered by the Higher Critics of the Bible as a fabricated composition of national songs of the Jews from the time of David to the time of Alexander of Macedon. No doubt some of these songs are the inspired compositions of David which are included in the Psalms of the Bible but they are very few. The Psalms which go in the name of David in the Old Testament belong to the latest of the Old Testament books. Some songs are of the Greek period. These include some 150 songs by various aurhors used as hymns in temple services attributed to David, Solomon, Asaph, Eithnan, Ezarite, Moses, and the sons of Korah, some songs belong to Moccbean times.

The songs of Dhaburah is now proved by the Higher criticism of the Bible to have originated in the time of David (eleventh century B.C.) and it is this song of Dhaburah which the Qur'an refers to as the Zabur of David. The Bible attributes this song to the prophetess Dhaburah (Hebrew for wasp) which cannot be true. As this song coincides with the time of David it is considered as the song sung by David when inspired by God. Some of these songs are included in the collection of songs called Psalms of David. The Qur'an has thus anticipated the Higher criticism of the Bible and instead of falling into the common error of confusing it with the so-called Psalms of David, called it by the name, "Zabur", a word familiar to the Jews but forgotten in respect of its contents and origin which were restored only by the Qur'an.

An instance of the judgment of David and Solomon is given into the Qur'an in the following verses. There is no mention of it in the Bible:

(3) And remember Da'ud and Sulaiman when they gave judgement concerning the field into which the sheep of certain people had strayed by night. We did witness their judgement. To Sulaiman We inspired the right understanding of the case. And to each of them We gave wisdom and knowledge and We constrained the mountains and the birds to join with Da'ud in celebrating Our praise. It was We who did it. (xxi. 78-79)

The commentators Baidawi and Jalaluddin give us the details of this judgment. It is reported that a ease of judgement was brought to David's court in which the sheep of a certain man on account of his negligence got into a cultivated field by night and ate up the young plants and tender shoots causing damage to the owner to the extent of a whole year's crop. Divid awarded the owner of the filed the sheep themselves in compensation for his damage. His son Solomon, a mere boy of eleven, though of a better decision which awarded a penalty fitting the offence best. The loss was the loss of the produce of the field. The corpus of the property was not lost. Solomon's suggestion was that the owner of the filed should not take the sheep altogether but only detain them long enough to recoup his actual damage from the milk, wool and the young ones of the sheep and then return the sheep to the owner.

David's merit was that he accepted the suggestion even though it came from a little boy. Solomon's merits was that he distinguished between corpus and income and though a boy, was not ashamed to put his case before his father. But in either case it was God who inspired the true realisation of justice. He was present and witnessed the affair as He is prevent everywhere.

David had the gift of song and sacred music as is manifested in his Psalms. All nature, hills birds sing and echo back the praises of God. The Qur'an makes mention of this in various places. For instance, in chapter xvii, verse 44 it says:

(4)   The seven heavens and the earth and all beings therein declare His glory. There is not a thing but celebrates His praise and yet ye understand not how they declare His glory. (xvii. 44)

And again in lvii. 1 and xiii. 13 the same fact is pointed out:

(5)   Whatever is in the heavens and on the earth declares the praise and glorifies God. (lvii. 1)

(6)   Nay the very thunder repeateth His praises. (xiii. 13)

In one of his songs in the collection of the Bible David also sings." Praise the Lord from the earth, ye....mountains and all the hills...creeping things and flying fowl." (148: 7-10) All nature sings to God's glory in unison with David and angels and men of God. It is to such songs that the Qur'an refers to:

(7)   We bestowed grace aforetime on Da'ud from Ourselves O ye mountains! Sing ye back the praises of Allah with him and ye birds also. (xxxiv. 10)

(8)   It was We that made the hills declare in unison with him Our praises at even tide and at the break of day and the birds (gathered in assemblies) all with him turned to Allah. (xxxviii. 18-19)

The special hours when the hills and groves echo the song of birds are in the evening and at dawn, when also the birds gather together, for, those are respectively their roosting hours and the hours of their concerted flight for the day.

David was also an adept craftsman. He used to make coats of mail with iron rings joined together on an extensive scale for his warriors as he had to fight many battles. The Qur'an refers to this also in the following verses:

(9) It was We who taught him the making of coats of mail
for your benefit, to guard you form each other's violence.
Will you then be grateful? (xxi. 80)

(10) And We made the iron soft for him (commanding) make
thou coats of mail balancing well the rings of chain-armour
and work ye righteousness. For, be sure I see what all ye
do. (xxxiv. 10-11)

Iron and steel are hard stuff but in the hands of a craftsman
they become soft and pliable to be turned into any shape and size.
The making of these coats of mail was for the defence of
righteousness. The manufacture of this defensive armour is
traditionally attributed to David. The first part of the last verse is
addressed to David who was the artificer of this defensive armour
but the second part is addressed to him and all his people, so that
they may be careful to see that they did not deviate from the path
of righteousness. Fighting is dangerous and may easily degenerate
into mere violence. They were to see that this should not happened
and they were told that God was watching over them all with the
personal solicitude implied in the singular pronoun I.

There is nothing but praise for David and his son Solomon in
the Qur'an. Mark these words of the Qur'an:

(11) We gave knowledge to Da'ud and Sulaiman and they both
said: Praise be to Allah who has favoured us above many
of his servants who believe. (xxvii. 15)

(12) Remember Our servant David, the man of strength. He
was frequent in returning to Allah. We strengthened his
kingdom and gave him wisdom and sound judgement in
speech and decision. (xxxviii. 17-20)

David and Solomon were both just men and apostles of God.
But the Bible on the one hand calls David "a man after God's own
heart" (I, Samuel, 13: 14) and on the other makes him a monster
of cruelty and injustice and full of lust as if God appreciate these
evils. Both father and son though so highly placed, were the Qur'an
says, never self-conceited. They always ascribed their knowledge,
wisdom and power to the only true source of all good, God.

Against this the Holy Bible gives an unholy story about David
in 2 Samuel, chapters 11 and 12, which tells us that David saw
the wife of Uriah, one of his warriors, washing herself in
nakedness. As she was beautiful he fell for her and sent for her

and committed adultery with her. When she conceived she sent word to David and David wanted her husband who returned from the battlefield, to go and lie with his wife so that she might cover her shame. But Uriah did not got to his wife and slept with David's servants. Then David sent him back to the battlefield with a letter addressed to his general Joab to put Uriah in the forefront of the combatants so that he may be killed. Joab obeyed and Uriah was slain and on learning that he was killed David usurped his wife. Then God sent Nathan the prophet to admonish David and he made David to judge himself by the parable of the ewe and David repented and God forgave him but the child of adultery died and David again lay with her and she gave birth to another son called Solomon who inherited the crown after him.

Is it not strange that according to Acts 13: 22 the Christians acclaim Christ as a son of David in spite of such horrible crime being attributed to him in the Old Testament which they believe to contain the inspired writings of the prophets of Israel. They should indeed feel grateful to the Holy Prophet of Islam who has done a great service to the prophets of God in absolving them of various charges that were levelled against them by their so called eclectic followers.

Some commentators have identified the episode of Uriah's wife with the vision of David which is given in 38: 21-26 under Jewish influence, but the majority of them have rejected it on the ground that David was a pious man and a prophet and he had a well-guarded private chamber for prayer and praise. The vision of David is described as follows:

> (13) Has the story of the disputants reached thee. When they climbed over the wall of the private chamber and entered the presence of Da'ud and he was terrified of them. They said: Fear not, we are two disputants, one of whom has wronged the other.
>
> Decide now between us with truth and treat us not with injustice but guide us to the even path. This man is my brother. He has ninety-nine ewes and I have only one and yet he says: commit her to my care, and is behaving harshly with me.
>
> Da'ud said: He has undoubtedly wronged thee in demanding thy (single) ewe to be added to his ewes; truly many are the

partners who wrong each other but those who believe and do good deeds do not do so, but they are very few.

And Da'ud gathered that We have tried him. He asked forgiveness of His Lord and fell down bowing and repentant. So We forgave him that; and surely he had access to Our presence and a beautiful place of (final) return.

O Da'ud! indeed make thee a vicegerent on earth. So judge thou between men in truth nor follow thou the lust of thy heart, for they will mislead thee from the path of Allah. For those who wander astray from the path of Allah is a grievous penalty for forgetting the day of Account. (xxviii. 21-26)

From the above account, if we take it literally that some enemies of David climbed the wall of his chamber to murder him but finding him awake pretended to present a dispute and demanded his verdict, them David with all his renowned sagacity and sense of judgement could have easily found out that there was no reason for the unjust brother to have come with the complainant risking his life in climbing the wall to evade the guard and to have said nothing in his own defence. Moreover, the time and the way in which they invaded the privacy of David by climbing over the wall would have certainly provoked him quite justly to call the guard and get them arrested for their untimely intrusion. But David did nothing of the sort, for, to his surprise they disappeared as mysteriously as they had come. It was then that David realised that it was a vision, a test of his moral and spiritual fibre, and a timely warning to protect him from falling into the pit of human frailty of even entertaining any lusty fancies about the woman who attracted his attention. Judged by the highest standard of those nearest of God, even the slightest deviation from the path of rectitude was an offence. As soon as this realisation came to him he fell down in humble prostration and turned to God in sincere repentance and this was therefore freely accepted by God.

The whole story is here different and the whole atmosphere is different from the parable of Nathan given in 2 Samuel, chapters 12 and 13. The fact is that the Bible never hesitates to narrate such scandalous crimes of the grossest character in respect of its prophets, because, presumably its writers had very low idea about prophets and their God.

Further on, in the same "Holy Script" chapter 13 we have the stories of rapes, incests, and fratricides in David's own household. Ammon the son of David raping his sister Tamar and Absalom her own brother avenging her honour by killing his brother Ammon, etc.

The Muslim idea of David is that of a man just and upright endowed will all the virtues that can be imagined to exist in a righteous man in whom even the slightest thought of any ill or self-relation gets immediately washed of by repentance and forgiveness.

XV

THE STORY OF THE PROPHET SULAIMAN (SOLOMON)

(May peace and blessings of Allah be on him)

Solomon was a son of David, and though not the eldest son, his father made him his heir, on account of the praiseworthy talents of his head and heart, and after him he ascended the throne of Judia. The Qur'an mentions it is in these words:

(1) The Da'ud We gave Sulaiman (for a son). How excellent in Our service and how frequently he turned to Us. (xxxviii. 30)

(2) And Sulaiman was Da'ud heir. (xxvii. 16)

Solomon not only inherited his father's kingdom but also his spiritual insight and the prophetic office which do not necesarily go from father to son. He was a great king and greater still because he served God and frequently turned to Him. The Qur'an unlike the Bible represents Solomon as a righteous king,not as an idolater doing "evil in the sight of the Lord" (1 Kings 11: 6).

(3) We gave knowledge to Da'ud and Sulaiman and they both said: Praise be to Allah who has favoured us above many of His believing servants. (xxvii. 15)

(4) To Sulaiman We inspired the right understanding of the case. To each of them We gave judgment and knowledge. (xxi. 79)

Solomon is mentioned in the Qur'an as a prophet along with several other prophets in iv. 163 and vi. 84. He was not only made a propeht but was also given, in response to his prayers, a kingdom and power such as was not given to any after him.[41]

---

41. His prayer is noted in the Qur'an in the following verse: "He said: my Lord! Forgive me and grant me a kingdom which may not belong to any after me, for, Thou art the Governer of bounties without measure," (xxxviii. 35)

(5) It was Our power that made the violent (untruly) wind flow (tamely) for Sulaiman to his order, to the land which We had blessed: for, We do know all things. (xxi. 81)

(6) Then We subjected the wind to his power to flow gently to his order whithersoever he willed. (xxxviii. 36).

(7) And (We made) the wind subservient to Sulaiman. It made a month's journey in the morning and a month's journey in the evening. (xxxiv. 12)

The significance of these verses is that by the command of God, Solomon could perform a journey of a month in a day or night as the wind had been made subservient to him. Can we doubt this today when we know that a pilot who flies an aeroplane traverses distances in a day or a night which otherwise could only be covered in a month or so. Again, the words "to the land We had blessed'' must refer to a land other than the Holy Land, for, Solomon was in fact ruling in Palestine already a Holy Land. Then which is that other blessed land to which the winds carried Solomon? The traditions of Kashmir about Solomon point clearly to it as being this blessed land which is called "Bagh-i-Jannat" or the garden of Paradise. This shows that Solomon did rule over an eastern country also other than palestine. There is a temple of Jewish design and plan on a hill in the vicinity of Srinagar which is called Takht-i-Sulaiman--the throne of Solomon. I had the opportunity to visit this place. This temple in design and construction is an exact replica of the tomb of Absalom, the son of David in the valley of Josephat (Palestine). There is a local tradition that king Solomon visited Kashmir by ari and rested on this hill. All Kashmiri historians have noted this tradition. European historians such as Bernier (1644), George Forster (1783), Vigne (1812), Mrs. Harvey (1854), Moore (1861), Col. Torrens (1862) and General Newall (1877) have noted this Kashmiri tradition about Solomon's coming by air and resting on this hill. And there are many Persian and Indian historians who have affirmed this

---

The answer to this prayer is given in the Bible in these words; Wisdom and knowledge is granted unto thee; and I will give thee riches, and wealth and honour, such as none of the kings have had that have been before thee, neither shall there any after thee have the like (2 Chronicles, 1: 12).

tradition in their own books. It may also be noted that there is a mountain peak called "Takht-i-Sulaiman" on the Hindukush mountains and tradition has it that Solomon had landed there also by air.

In addition to this extraordinary achievement Solomon was gifted with a knowledge of birds' voices. The Qur'an testifies to it in these words:

> (8) He (Sulaiman) said: O ye people! we have been taught the speech of birds and on us has been bestowed a little of all things, This is indeed Grace manifest (from Allah). (xxvii. 10)[42]

Though spoken word in human speech is different from the means of communication which birds and animals have among themselves, no man can doubt that they have means of communication with one another, if he only observes the orderly fight of migratory birds or the regulated behaviour of ants, bees and other creatures who live in communites. The wisdom of Solomon partly consisted in understanding their communications. He had something of all desirable gift and with true gratitude he referred them to God, the Giver of all gifts.

Among his special gifts was also the power over the jinns and the devils who worked for him:

> (9) And before Sulaiman were marshalled his hosts--of jinns and men and birds and they were all in order and ranks. (xxvii. 17)

> (10) And of the devils were some who dived for him and did other works besides and it was We who guarded them. (xxi. 82)

> (11) And there were Jinns who worked in front of him by the leave of his Lord, and if any of them turned aside from Our comamnd We made him taste of the penalty of the blazing fire. They worked for him as he desired, making arches, images, basins as large as reservoirs and cooking cauldrons, fixed in their places. (xliv. 12-13)

The Jinns and devils mentioned in the above verses were

---

42. In 1 Kings 4: 33 it is said: "He spake also of beasts, and fowls, and of creeping things and of fishes." This shows that Solomon was given the wisdom to understand the ways of all living creatures of God.

subjected to Solomon to help him in the building of the temples.[43] This was a special favour granted by God to Solomon in response to his prayers which no other king enjoyed after him: "Grant me a kingdom which may not belong to any after him" (xxxviii. 35)

Solomon was also a great lover of horses and he was himself a great equestrian. But this love was not like that of a mere race-goer or of a warrior. There was a spiritual element in it--the love of the highest good. He had great armies and wealth but he used them all in God's service. His battles were not fought for lust of blood but as "Jihads" in the cause of righteousness. The Qur'an speaks of this in these words:

(12) Behold! They were brought before him at eventide coursers of the highest breeding and swift of foot and he said: Truly do I love the good with a view to the glory of my Lord, until they were out of sight. (He said): Bring them bach to me. Then he began to stroke their ankles and decks. (xxxviii, 31-33)

Horses are always stroked on their legs and necks after a race. It was this that Solomon did in approbation of their high speed, for they had gone so far in the race that they were quickly out of his sight. But the commentators have twisted these words into a purile story that Solomon, enraged on account of the horses having detained him from his afternoon prayer, began to cut off their legs and necks as if it were the fault of the horses and not

---

43. "Demons obeyed him (Solomon)...and evil spirits were subjected to him" (*Jewish Targum on Esther*, 1, 2). These Targums were mostly in Aramaic and the Prophet knew nothing of Aramic language. If this aspect of Solomon's power was a mere invention of the Prophet's mind, the Jews would not have kept silent but would have accused the Prophet of inventing false stories which have no reference in their scriptures. But among the Jews who embraced islam during the Prophet's lifetime were men of learning like 'Abdullah bin Salam They never raised any objections to these revelations of the Prophet which belong to the Meccan period. On the other hand they became more convinced of the Divine inspiration of the Prophet. There is another interpretation of the words Jinn and Shayatin as hardy non-Israelite tribes subjugated by Solomon who were employed in the building of the temple. But these words are widely used in the Qur'an side by side with men (as can be seen in quotation No. 9) and therefore there is no justification to call them as hardy non-Israelite tribes.

his own fault. The words of the Qur'an do not indicate that Solomon neglected any prayer in reviewing his horses nor do they say that he cut off their legs and necks, neither is there any mention of the son going into the veil of night. This incident is mentioned in the Qur'an to show that like Solomon the prophet will also have to make use of horses in the service of God.

> (13) And indeed We made Sulaiman pass through an ordeal and placed on his throne (for a while) a mere body but he did turn to Us (in repentance) he said: O my Lord! Forgive me, for, Thou art the Granter of bounties without measure. (xxviii 34-35)

What was the ordeal through which Solomon laid to pass? The commentorators have given different version in the explanation of these verses. But all these seem to be quite wide to mark and are based on no authentic record. Most of these are mere conjectures. From a study of the account of Solomon given in the book of the Old Testament (though most of their contents are unreliable) it appears that some of the trusted servants of Solomon were unbelievers and idol-worshippers. One of these was Jeroboam whom Solomon had made the governor of the northern districts of his realm. He was an idol-worshipper, for, when he got power he set up calf worship. He conspired against Solomon and rebelled against him and before Solomon could get scent of it he attacked Jerusalem and by mere brute force occupied the throne of Solomon. But he was neither a statesman nor a man of understanding. Solomon though displaced in the moment of his unawarness, form his throne, did not lose heart and he raillied all his faithful servants and expelled Jeroboam from Jerusalem, the seat of his government. It is to this conspiracy that the Bible alludes in these words:

> Solomon sought therefore to kill Jeroboam. And Jeroboam arose, and fled into Egypt, unto Shishak king of Egypt, and was in Egypt until the death of Solomon. (I Kings, 11: 40)

During the weak reign of Rehoboam, the son of Solomon, Jeroboam returned to Jerusalem and again assumed power. Note the version of the Bible:

> And it came to pass, when all Israel heard that Jeroboam was come again, that they sent and called him into the

congregation, and made him king over all Israel: there was none that followed the house of David, but the tribe of Judah only. (I Kings 12: 29)

It was this incident in the life of Solomon that the Qur'an refers in the above verses, that Solomon had to pass through an ordeal, but as he always turned to God and sought His forgiveness for the slight negligence of his kingly duties, he was given back his kingdom, and in response to his prayer for the grant of a kingdom he was given the power over the forces of nature, over the Jinns and devils and the birds and other living creatures. It is to these bounties that the Qur'an refers in the following verses:

(14) Such are Our bounties, whether thou bestow them on others or withhold them, no account will be asked of thee. And he enjoyed a near approach to Us and a beautiful place of (final) return. (xxxviii, 39-40)

An account of these bounties is further given in the following verses:

(15) At length when they came to a valley of ants[44] one of the ants said: O ye ants! get into your habitations lest Sulaiman and his hosts crush you without knowing it. Thereupon, he smiled (amused) at her speech and he said: O my Lord! So order me that I may be grateful for Thy favours which Thou hast bestowed on me and on my father, and that I may work the righteousness, that will please Thee, and admit me by Thy grace into the ranks of Thy righteous servants. (xxvii. 18-19)

These verses suggest the symbolical meaning as predominant. The ant, to all outward appearance, is a very small and humble creature. In the great pomp and splendour of the world, she may be neglected or even trampled on by a people who mean her no harm. Yet by her wisdom she carries on her own life within her own sphere unmolested and makes a useful contribution to the economy

---

44. The word "Naml" translated ant was also the name of tribe who occupied the territory between Jibrin and 'Asqalan and formed like a buffer State between Solomon and the Queen of Saba' (as interpreted by Maulana Muhammad Ali in his Commentary). But the word as given in the verses conveys a different idea. We have, therefore, followed the literal meaning of the world "Naml".

of the world. So there is room for the humblest people in the spiritual world.

The counterpart of the position of the humble ant is the position of a great king like Solomon. He prays that his power and wisdom and all other gifts may be used for righteousness and for the benefit of all around him. The ant being in his thoughts he means particularly in his prayers that he may not even unwittingly tread on humble beings in his pre-occupations with the great things of the world.

In the Kingdom of God righteousness is the badge of citizenship and the base of that citizenship is the universal brotherhood of righteousness. The greatest in that kingdom are glad and proud to pray for that essential badge.

The Qur'an then narrates the story of Solomon's intercourse with the Queen of Saba'. This queen can be identified with the Biblical Queen of Sheba (I Kings, 1-10) but the story related here is not found in the Bible but is contained in the Targum referred to in footnote 3, of course with slight variation to impress the spritiual lessons which are conspicuous by their absence in all Jewish literature. The Jewish Rabbis of the Prophet's time knew it well. To say that the Prophet adopted this story from these Tarugms, as Rodwell suggests, cannot be accepted for the same reasons as have already been given under the same footnote. Here is what the Qur'an says:

> (16) And he reviewed the birds, and then said: How is it I see not Hudhud or is it that he is of the absentees[45] I will

---

45. Hudhud (literal meaning; Lapowing or Hoopoe) is taken by the Commentators as a bird in the army of Solomon. This idea aries from the fact that his name is mentioned in connection with the review of birds. But it is difficult to consider him as a bird from what he has said about the Queen of Saba'. Only a man could judge what a false belief or a wicked deed was It is beyond the ken of a bird. Further, the infliction of severe punishment on a small bird by such a might monarch as Solomon and the exposition of the great religious doctrine of Unity by a bird, are quite incomprehensible. It must be a man whose name was Hudhud and who must have been an officer of the Intelligence Department of Solomon's army. Such names are not unusual, for we find in I Kings 20: 1 a king of Syria called Ben-Hudhud. The Arab writers speak of a king of Himyar as Hudhud which is almost identical with Hudhud mentioned in the Qur'an.

most certainly chastise him with a severe chastisement or
kill him or he shall bring to me a clear plea. But Hudhud
did not tarry long. He then (came up and) said: I have
compassed territory which thou hast not compassed and
I have come to thee from Saba' with sure information I
found a woman ruling over them and she has been given
of everything, and she has a magnificent throne. I found
her and her people worshiping the sun instead of Allah
and the devil has made their deeds fair-seeming to them
and has kept them away from the right path. So, they are
misguided, as they do not make obeisance to Allah who
brings to light what is hidden in the heavens and the earth
and knows what you hide and what you reveal. Allah!
there is no god but He. He is the Lord of Mighty power.
(xxvii. 18-26)

Saba' was a city in Yemen about fifty miles from the city of
Sana'a. A recent German explorer, Dr Hans Hel Fritz claim to have
located it in what is now Hadramaut territory. The famous dam
of Ma'arib made the country very prosperous and enabled it to
attain a high degree of civilisation. The Abyssinians posses a
traditional history called *Kebra Nagast* (the Book of the Glory of
Kings) which has been translated from the Ethiopic into English
by Sir E.A. Wallis Budge (Oxford, 1932) in which a full accont of
the queen of Sheba and her son is given who is considered to be
the founder of the Abyssinian Dynasty.

The ancient religion of the people of Saba' consisted in the
worhsip of the heavenly bodies, the sun, the planets and the stars.
The false worship of these Sabbaans is here exposed in three ways:
(1) that they were self-satisfied with their own human achievements
instead of looking up to God; and (2) that the light of the heavenly
bodies which they worrshipped was dependent only on the true
light of God which extends over heaven and earth; the Creator
should be worshipped rather than His creation; and (3) God knows
the hidden secrets of man's minds as well as the objects which
they openly profess:

(17) Sulaiman said: soon shall we see if thou hast told the truth
or thou art of the liars. Go thou with this letter of mine
and deliver it to them and turn away from them and see
what answer they return.

She said: Ye chiefs! Here is delivered to me a letter worthy of respect. It is from Sulaiman and is (as follows): In the name of Allah, the Beneficent, the Merciful. Be ye not arrogant against me but come to me in submission. She said: Ye cheifs! Advise me in this my affair, for, I never decide an affair until you are in my presence.

They said: We are endowed with strength and are possessors of mighty powers, but the command is thine. Therefore see what thou wilt command.

She said; Kings, when they enter a town despoil it and make the noblest of its people the meanest, Thus do they behave. But I am going to send a present to them and shall wait to see what answer do the messengers bring back. (xxvii. 27-35)

The character of the queen as disclosed here is that of a ruler enjoying great wealth and dignity and the full confidence of her subjects. She does nothing without consulting her council and her council are ready to carry out her command in all things. Her peopel are manly, loyal, and contended and ready to take the field against any enemy of thier country. But their queen is prudent and not willing to embroil her country in war. She has the discrimination to see that Solomon is not liek ordinary kings who conquer by violence. She thinks that an exchange of presents would probably establish better relations between the two kingdoms. In her we have a picture of womanhood, gentle, and able to tame the wilder passions of her subjects:

(18) Now, when (the ambassador) came to Sulaiman he (Sulaiman) said: What! will you give me abundance in wealth? But what Allah has given me is better than that which He has given you. Nay, it is ye who are exultant because of your presents. Go back to them and be sure we shall come to them with such hosts as they will never be able to meet We shall expel them from there in disgrace and they will feel humbled indeed. (xxvii. 36-37).

The queen thought she had arranged with womanly tact to conciliate Solomon and at the same time pacify her warlike subjects. But Solomon took it as an insult that she should send him presents instead of her submission to the true faith. He, therefore, flung back the presents at her:

> (19) He said (to his own men): Ye chiefs! which of you can
> bring me her throne before they come to me in submission.
> One audacious among the Jinns said: I will bring it to thee
> before thou rise from thy palce. Indeed I am strong and
> can be trusted. But one who had the knowledge of the
> Book said: I will bring it to thee in the twinkling of an
> eye. Then when Sulaiman saw it placed firmly before him,
> he said: This is by the grace of my Lord to test me whether
> I am grateful or ungrateful. And if any is grateful truly
> his gratitude is (again) for his own self. But if any is
> ungrateful, my Lord is Self-Sufficient, Honoured. He said:
> Transform her throne out of all recognition by her. Let us
> see if she is guided (to the truth) or is one of those who
> receive no guidance. (xxvii. 38-41)

Solomon was thankful to God that he had men endowed with
such power who could transport to his court the queen's throne
and transform it as he desired without the queen even knowing
it.

Man's gratitude to God is not a thing that benefits God, for
God is high above all needs. It benefits a man's own self and gives
him higher rank in the spiritual world and men's ingratitude will
not detract from God's glory or Honour or the value of God's
generous gifts to man, for, God is supreme in Honour, Glory and
Generosity:

> (20) So, when she arrived she was asked: Is this thy throne?
> She said: It was just like this and we were given the
> knowledge before it, and we were (already) submissive and
> he diverated her from the worship of otehrs besides Allah,
> for, she was sprung of a people that have no faith.
> She was asked to enter the lofty palace, but when she saw
> it, she thought it was a lake of water and she tucked up
> her skirts uncovering her legs.
> He said: This is but a palace paved smooth with slabs of
> glass. She said: O my Lord! I have indeed wronged myself;
> I do submit with Sulaiman to the Lord of the worlds. (xxvii
> 42-45)

The queen having been received with honour on her arrival
and having accepted the transformation of her throne was asked

to enter the great palace itself. Its floor was made of slabs of smooth polished glass that glistened like water. She thought it was water and trucked up her skirts to pass through it, showing her bare feet and ankles.

This was a very undignified position for a woman specially one of the position of a queen. Solomon immediately undecieved her and told her the real facts when she felt grateful and joined herself with Solomon in praising God.

This was meant to teach her a lesson how wrong she was to worships outward objects such as the sun while the real force or the source of life was God whose hand worked in these objects.

Among the propehts of the Israelites after Moses, David and Solomon are given the greatest prominence in the Qur'an, and the glory to which the Israelite kingdom arose under these prophet-kings is referred to on more occasions than one. In fact all this is history containing the prophecy of the greatness of Islam. The chapters containing such references are those which were revealed at Mecca when opposition to the Prophet was at its highest and his cause seemed to be quite hopeless. The narration of this history was a comfort to the Muslims that the time was coming when all opposition to the Propeht would be brought to naught and Islam would shine forth in all its glory and that the Holy Prophet was destined to occupy both the position of a spiritual world-teacher and a king like David and Solomon.

With all the glory that is attributed to Solomon his death was also a death knell of his kingdom and his successor was only "a worm of the earth that ate away his staff," the reference being to the life of ease and luxury which Rehoboam, his son led, "the eating away of the staff" indicating the disruption of his kingdom.

(21) Then, when We decreed Sulaiman's death, nothing showed them his death except a little worm of the earth which kept slowly gnawing away at his staff. So when he fell down, the Jinns saw plainly that if they had known the unseen, they would not have tarried in the humiliating penalty (of their task). (xxxiv 14)

The commentators, to explain the above passage, have given a story here which does not stand to criticism for a single moment.

The story runs as follows: David having laid the foundation of the temple of Jerusalem left it to be finished by his son solomon who employed the Jinns in the work. Before the edifice was quite completed, perceiving his end drawing near, Solomon begged of God that his death might be concealed from the Jinns till they had entirely finished it. God therefore so ordered it that Solomon died as he stood at his prayer leaning on his staff which suported the body in this posture for a full year. And the Jinns supposing him to be alive continued their work during that term, at the expiration of which the temple being perfectly completed, a worm, which had been gnawing the staff from inside, ate it through and the corpse fell to the ground disclosing the king's death.

There is no authority to support this story anywhere either in the Bible or the Talmud, or the traditions of the Holy Prophet. Besides, was it not strange that no one during the course of a year discovered that Solomon was neither eating nor moving nor answering the calls of nature nor looking after the affairs of the kingdom (for he was not only a prophet but a powerful king surrounded by powerful foes) but standing in one place as a statue and that too with the suport of a single staff (which it cannot possibly make a corpse to stay on in an erect posture). Moreover, would not this be an act of sacrilege to leave the dead body of a propeht and a king unburied for so long a time? And after all what was the purpose of bringing such a fable here in the context of Saba' and its people who were destroyed by flood for their iniquities.

The verses that follow show that when people behaved ungratefully to God by not making use of their talents and their wealth for the defence of righteousness, they are deprived of their felicities and reduced to naught. This is plainly hinted at in the verse preceding the verse under reference: "Work ye sons of Dawud! with thanks, but few of My servants are grateful." (xxxiv. 13)

The fact is that the Qur'an illustrates the fall of Solomon's empire by an allegory, calling his son "a worm of the earth that ate away his staff", for under him the kingdom of Solomon went to pieces Rehoboam who succeeded Solomon led a life of luxury and ease and instead of acting on the advice of the older men he yielded to the pleasure-seeking wishes of his companions (1 Kings, 12: 13), and it is to these luxurious habits and easy mode of life that the Qur'an refers when it calls him a "worm of the earth".

The eating away of the staff signifies the disruption of his kingdom. Those who were reduced to subjection, including the Jinns, regained their liberty.

This as well as story of the people of Saba' which follows is brought in here as a warning to the Muslims against the result of falling into luxury and ease, by which, however, they benefited very little. The ultimate fate of the kingdoms of the Umayyads and the Abbasids was the same as that of Solomon's.

Now before closing this chapter, let us turn to the Bible and see that even an illustrious king like Solomon was not spared from being blasphemed. We read the following remarks about Solomon in the Bible: "For it came to pass, when Solomon was old, that his wives turned away his heart after other gods" (1 Kings 11: 4) and that "the Lord was angry with Solomon, because his heart was turned from the Lord God of Israel." (1 Kings, 11: 9)

How preposterous that a prophet of God who is in constant touch with the Almighty God should be so faithless to his Lord. Evidently this is a figment of a filthy imagination. The Qur'an refutes this charge when it says:

(22) And they follow that which the devils fabricated against Sulaiman's kingdom and Sulaiman did not disbelieve but the devils disbelieved, teaching men enchantment. (ii. 102)

It is not otherwise established that the statement of the Bible is wrong in this respect. The Rev. T.K. Cheyne shows conclusively in *The Encyclopaedia Biblica* (col. 4689) that Solomon was not a polytheist and having shown how mistakes crept into the Bible he concludes: "That Solomon has a number of wives both Israelites and non-Israelites, is probable enough, but he did not make altars for all of them nor did he himself combine the worship of his wives' gods with that of Yehwe."

It this not a standing miracle of the Qur'an that the truths revealed by it to the world fourteen centuries back are being corroborated one after another by the researches of modern scholars?

XVI

THE STORY OF THE PROPHETS ZACHARIAH AND YAHYA (JOHN THE BAPTIST)

(May peace and blessings of Allah be on them)

Prophet Zachariah

Zachariah is mentioned in the Qur'an as a prophet along with several other prophets in vi. 86. But a special mention of him praying to God for a son is made in three places followed by an account of the birth of Jesus:

(1) There did Zachariah pray to his Lord, saying: My Lord! Grant me from Thee a good offspring, for surely Thou art He that heareth prayer. Then the angels called him as he stood praying in the sanctuary. They said: Allah gives thee the good news of Yahya testifying to the truth of a word from Allah and honourable, and chaste, and a prophet from among the righteous.

He said: My Lord! How shall there be a son born to me since old age has come upon me and my wife is barren? Even thus doth Allah what he pleases, was the answer. He said: My Lord! Give me a sign. The sign shall be (said they) that thou shouldst not speak to men for three days except by signs and remember your Lord much and glorify Him in the evening and the morning. (iii. 37-40)

The same incident is narrated in another place with greater detail:

(2) (This is) a recital of mercy of the Lord to His servant Zachariah, when he called upon his Lord in secret. He said: My Lord! Surely my bones are weakened and my head flares with hoariness and my Lord! I have never been unblest in my prayer to Thee. Surely I fear what my cousins will do after me, and my wife is barren; therefore grant me from Thyself an heir who would represent me and

represent the progeny of Ya'qub and make him, my Lord, one with whom Thou art well-pleased (His prayer was answered) O Zachariah! Surely We give thee good news of a boy whose name shall be Yayha. We have not caused any to bear the same name before him. He said: O my Lord! How shall I have a son when my wife is barren and I am quite decrepit from old age. He said: So shall it be. Thy Lord says, it is easy to Me and indeed I created thee before when thou hadst been nothing. He said: My Lord! Give me a sign. Thy sign, said He, shall be that thou shouldst speak to no man for three nights although thou art not dumb.

So he went forth to his people from the sanctuary, then, he made known by signs to them that they should glorify Allah morning and evening. (xix. 2-11)

(3) And remember Zachariah when he cried to his Lord: O my Lord! Leave me not without an offspring though Thou art the best of inheritors. So We responded to him and gave him Yahya and made his wife fit for him. Surely they used to hasten, one with another, in deeds of goodness and called upon Us hoping and fearing and they were humble before Us. (xxiii. 89-90)

Zachariah was a priest attached to the temple dedicated to God. His relatives were his colleagues but he found in them no true spirit of the service of God and man, and he feared that his family and relatives were going wrong. He wanted to keep the lamp of God burning bright. He was, therefore, filled with anxiety about his office after him. He was not anxious to have a son to satisfy a mere human desire for ones progeny; if it has been so, he would have prayed much earlier in his life when he was a young man. He was too full of true piety to put merely selfish things into his prayer. But here was public need for the service of the Lord that he should have a good successor. He had no worldly property for his heir to inherit, but he had character and virtue as a man of God and this he wanted to transmit to his heir as the most previous possession of the posterity of Jacob. The people around him had fallen away from the path of God. His heir like him might try to win them back to God's service. These were his thoughts while he prayed to his Lord for a good and pure offspring and his wish was granted. God removed the defect of his wife's barrenness so that she could become mother and she gave birth to Yahya who is called "honourable, chaste and a prophet from among the righteous".

The sign was not given in order to convince Zachariah that God's promise was true for, he had full faith in God, but it was a symbol by which he was to show in his conduct that he was to conform to his new destiny as the father of Yahya who was to take up the work and Zachariah was to come. Yahya was to take up the work and Zachariah was to be silent although there was no physical defect preventing him from speaking. The asking for a sign and its being given also served the purpose of satisfying him that the good news given to him by the angel came really from God and it was no sort of delusion.

The Qur'an does not say that Zachariah was made dumb. But the Bible makes Zachariah mute during the whole period from the time of the announcement of the birth of a son to his actual birth as a punishment for a question which, according to the Bible, implied unbelief.

> And, behold, thou shalt be dumb, and not able to speak, until the day that these things shall be performed, because thou believest not my words, which shall be fulfilled in the season. (Luke, 1: 20)

This again is an instance of a libel against the prophet of God charging him with unbelief in the word of God. The question cannot be understood as disbelief. It was put just to know how he would beget a son when the usual requisites of begetting children were absent, God chose just to say that He would give him a son and he was satisfied. It is the ordinary mentality of common mortals to think in the way in which the writers of the Bible have thought.

The Prophet Yahya (John the Baptist)

(4) (To his son came the command) O Yahya![46] (Take hold

---

46. The name Yahya which is used in the Qur'an is not one of the various forms of John It is quite different--rather the Armenians consider this name to be another form of Elijah, Yeghiya. But the more revealing fact is that in the sacred books of Mandeans or the Christians of John the Baptist a sect still found in Iraq and undoubtedly older than Islam,

of the Book firmly. And We granted him wisdom even as a youth and tenderness (for all creatures) from Us and purity and he was devout and dutiful to his parents and he was not overbearing nor disobedient. So, peace on him the day he was born, and the day he dies, and the day he will be raised up to life. (xix. 12-15)

Yahya was granted wisdom even as a youth for the boldly denounced sin. He was given gentle pity and love for all God's creatures and he moved among the humble and the lowly; he despised soft raiment. He is known for the purity of the life that he lived. He spent most of his life in wilderness. All the work that he turned out was in his youth. He was devout showing love to God and God's creatures and more particularly to his parents. The Bible narrates that he did not live long. He was imprisoned by Herod, the Roman governor of Judea, whom he had reproved for his sins and eventually beheaded at the instigation of the women with whom Herod was infatuated.

> Jesus who came after him is reported to have said about him: Verily I say unto you, Among them that are born of women there hath not risen a greater than John the Baptist. (Matt 11: 11: Luke, 7:28)

John is called with the special epithet attached to his name, "The Baptist" as he used to baptise people. This ceremony among the Jews was performed on reaching a certain age. Till then strict observance of the Law was not demanded. Minority of age was taken as responsible for all defaults. But after baptism fulfilment of all righteousness was expected. We use water in cleansing things from all impurities. We wash ourselves to remove all physical uncleanliness from our body. So a Jew was plunged into a tank or river at him baptism to signify that he had purged himself of his past impurities--moral and spiritual--and prepared for a new life. This symbolism worked well among the primitive people when their mind was in its infancy and worked under superstition. With the growth of culture and knowledge it should have given way to the great verities of life.

---

we find this prophet is named Yahya and not Yahannah (the Habrew form of John) which as common a name amongst the Jews as John is amongst the Christians, but the Qur'an says that it was a name never borne by any Jew before yahya the son of Zachariah (xix.7)

But the Christian Church uses this ceremony of Baptism to symbolise the new dispensation in fulfilment of a prophecy of John the Baptist which runs thus:

> I indeed baptize you with water unto repentance: but he that cometh after me is mightier than I, whose shows I am not worthy to bear: he shall baptize you with the Holy Ghost and with fire (Matt., 3: 11)

The Christians take these words to apply to Jesus but the ceremony is not performed with fire as given in the above prophecy. Jesus and his Church never made use of fire when initiating people into their fold. This leads one to believe that the Baptist did not allude to the son of Mary but to someone else for the full application to the word in the above quotation.

As this chapter is devoted to Yayha (John the Baptist) we have taken the liberty to digress a little from our main subject, "the stories as given in the Qur'an," to the question of Baptism and the Prophecy of John the Baptist about one who shall baptise with the Holy Ghost and with fire.

Sabagh is the Arabic equivalent for the word Baptism. It literally means to dip a thing into a dye. The Qur'an says:

(5) (Receive) the baptism of Allah and who is better than Allah is baptising and Him do we serve. (ii. 138)

Baptism or the colour of God is Islam. When we dip a thing into dye it loses its original colour and assumes a new one. 'The object of baptism is the same--to be at one with God and to walk humbly with Him. We cannot attain to this spiritual state unless we lose our own colour and adopt that of God. John the Baptist meant the same thing when he referred to baptism with fire. When a thing is put in the fire it apparently loses its own entity and assumes the colour and attributes of fire. Divine baptism is to plunge into the spiritual fire to consume our own entity and to be like a dead person in the hand of God, with no personal will, or exercise of our own discretion, but absolute submission to His will and implicit obedience to His commandments. This is the literal meaning of Islam. Hence the words of the Qur'an which say "Islam is the baptism of God". Thus we find in Islam the true interpretation of the words of John the Baptist.

The Baptist spoke simple truth when he said: "I indeed baptize you with water unto repentance." If we wish to get a dye properly on a cloth we cannot do so unless our cloth is perfectly clean of all spots. If not, we have to wash it with water before dipping it into the dye. So says John. You have to wash your unclean spiritual linen with the water of repentance before you plunge into the fire, the day of God. Where is that fire of God which may burn our dross and give us its own colour and attributes?

In order to answer these questions we should first try to find the elements our "Self" that constitute chiefly our entity. It is our will, our discretion, and our judgment. They give us our independent entity and differentiate us from the universe. When we subordinate our will to that of the other, morally speaking, we lose our very existence. It is not more difficult to plunge into burning fire than to yield completely to the opinions of others. To baptise ourselves with fire, therefore, is to immolate our will before the will of God, and this means Islam. Hence the Qur'anic text: "Islam is the Baptism of God." Baptism with water is a preparation for baptism with fire.

We all are more or less self-willed. Our will requires training and discipline. Besides, unless we have the revealed will of God before us, we have nothing to be subordinate to. In every hour of our life we have to use our will. Unless there are two courses before us, one dictated by our own will and the other prescribed by God, there is no occasion for us to subordinate our will to that of God. To reach that high state of resignation to the Will of God, we require a course of discipline, a training under which we have to learn how to win the victory for God in the daily struggle of our life, between our will and that of the most High and between our discretion and desire and those of the Almighty. We do need the Law and external guidance.

To bring complete death on our passions and desires is the baptism with fire. If we succeed in doing so, we are in a position to imbue ourselves with Divine attributes, this being baptism with the Holy Ghost. Like an iron in the fire, we lose our own colour and attributes and become like fire. Heat emanates from us and we perform all its functions. When that stage is reached God becomes as our limbs and our joints; our hands are His hands, our eyes are His eyes, and our feet are His feet. We work wonders and perform miracles because the will of God works through us. History records that Islam has produced men of such calibre and they have worked miracles, men who were baptised with the Holy Ghost and with fire and had dyed themselves in the colour of God.

XVII

OTHER PROPHETS MENTIONED IN THE QUR'AN

(Peace and blessings of Allah be on all of them)

There are several other prophets whose names are mentioned in the Qur'an but there are no stories concerning them. They are Elias, Elisha. Dhul-Kifl, Idris, and Uzair.

The Prophet Elias

About Elias the Qur'an says:

(1) And Elias was most surely of the apostles. When he said to his people: Will you not fear (the punishment of) Allah? What! Do you call upon Baal and forsake the best of creators, Allah, your Lord, and the Lord of your fathers of yore? But they called him a liar and therefore they shall most surely be brought up (for punishment) except the sincere and devoted servants of Allah. And He perpetuated for him praise among the later generations. Peace be on such as Elias. Even thus do We reward the doers of good. Surely he was one of Our believing servants. (xxxvii. 123-132)

Elias is mentioned as one of the prophets in vi. 86 also. He is the same as Elijah of the Bible whose story is given in the Bible in 1 Kings, 17-19 and 2 Kings 1-11. His people worshipped the Sun-God Baal. He had to flee for his life and eventually he disappeared mysteriously, but according to the Bible he was taken up in a whirlwind to heavens in a chariot of fire (2 Kings, 2: 11). The Jews still except him to descend from the heavens and thus converted the whole episode to a myth.

The Prophet Elisha

He is mentioned once only by name in vi. 86, along with

Ishmael, Jonah, and Lot--all four being stated as excelling the world.

The Prophet Dhul-Kifl

He is identified with Ezekile of the Bible who was carried away to Babylon after the destruction of Jerusalem. He was chained and bound and put into prison. He bore all with patience and constancy and continued boldly to reprove the evils in Israel. He is mentioned along Ishmael and Idris in the Qur'an.

(2) All were men of constancy and patience. We admitted them into Our mercy, for they were of the righteous ones. (xxi. 85-86).

(3) And commemorate Isma'il, Elias, and Dhul-Kifl. Each of them was of the company of the good. (xxxviii. 48)

The Prophet Idris

(4) Also mention in the Book the case of Idris. He was a man of truth and a prophet, and We raised him to a lofty station. (xix. 56)

The Prophet 'Uzair

He is mentioned in the Qur'an only once in ix. 30:

(5) And the Jews say: 'Uzair is the son of Allah.

Among the Israelite prophets 'Uzair was specially honoured and the Talmudists use very exaggerated language about him. A certain section of the Jews even called him the Son of God.

The Prophet Joshua

He is not mentioned by name but is referred to in v. 23.

The Prophet Samuel

He is also not mentioned by name but is referred to in ii. 246 to 248 in connection with the appointment of Saul as the king of the Israelites.

And this finishes the list of prophets mentioned in the Qur'an. But there are many more prophets whose names have not been mentioned in the Qur'an.

(6) Of some apostles We have told thee the story, of others
We have not. (iv. 164).

Of all the religions of the world Islam is the only one that laid
down the broad basis of faith in all the prophets of the world and
made it one of the principal of doctrines of the faith of Islam.

(7) Who believe in that which was revealed before thee (ii.
4) includes revelation to all the nations of the world, for
we are told that:

(8) There is not a people but a warner has gone among them.
(xxxv. 24).

XVIII

OTHER STORIES OF THE QUR'AN

1. The Story of Haurt and Marut

(1) And when apostle came to them from Allah confirming that which was with them, some of them to whom it was given threw the scriptures of Allah behind their back as if they knew it not. And they acted upon what the evil ones (among them) fabricated against the prophethood of Sulaiman. And Sulaiman never committed heresy; it was these devils who were heretical, teaching sorcery to people. Besides, neither was anything sent down in Babel to any angles called Harut and Marut, nor did they ever teach anyone saying: We are there to try you, so do not turn unbelievers. Still they went on learning from (the supposed) two (sources) what was considered to cause division between man and wife. But they certainly could harm none unless Allah so willed. And these people have learnt only what harmeth them and not what profiteth, and assuredly they knew that whoever purchases it (art of sorcery) has no share in the life to come, verily for a vile price they have sold themselves. Would that they knew it. Had they believed and acted righteously, they would have received from God a good recompense. Would that they knew it. (ii. 101-103)

Among the Jewish traditions in the Midrash (Jewish Commentary) was a story of two angels who asked of God permission to come down to earth but succumbed to temptation and were hung up by their feet at Babylon by way of punishment. Such stories about sinning angels who were cast down were believed in by the early Christians also (see the second Epistle of Peter, 11; 4 and Epistle of Jude, 5:6). Sale in his notes on these verse says that the Persian Magi "mention two rebellious angels of the same name now hung up by their feet with heads downwards in the territory of Bible." He further adds: "The Jews have something of this of the angel Shamhozal who having debauched himself with women repented and by way of penance hung himself up between heavens and earth."

Upon these two names lengthy fables are built up by some commentators. But the Qur'an does not contain a word about these stories. It plainly discredits them by denying that sorcery was revealed to any angels. For angels do not have free intercourse with human beings and they are not sent to men so as to live among them and teach them anything. The functions that are attributed to angels in the Qur'an convey no such ideas.

The statement made by the Qur'an in these verses amounts to this: the Jews instead of following the world of God followed certain evil crafts which they falsely attributed to Solomon and Harut and Marut, the two supposed angels of Babel. Solomon is declared free of any such sinfulness attributed to him and the story of the two angels is declared to be a fabrication, and that by these crafts they cannot inflict and injury on the Holy Prophet or the believers. Similar words are met with in Chap. lviii. Where, after denouncing the secret counsels of the enemies of Islam, it is said in verse 10: "Secret counsels are only the work of the devil that he may cause to grieve those who believe but he cannot hurt them in the least except with Allah's permission."

The reference here is to the secret counsels which were carried on by the Jews against the Holy Prophet. Here the Jews are spoken of as following the devil while ascribing there evil ways to prophets and angels. The Qur'an asserts that they cannot profit by such vile methods.

Imam Razi in his commentary, after mentioning the stories appended to the names Harut, and Marut, says that these stories are false and constitute a calumny against angels. Imam Baidavi also states that this story is based on Jewish sources. In the commentary of Mazhari it is stated that there is no tradition on this subject in the Traditions of the Prophet, both authentic and spurious.

II. The Story of the Two Sons of Adam

(2) And relate to them the story of the two sons of Adam with truth, when they both presented an offering. It was

accepted from one of them and was not accepted from the other. He said: Be sure, I will slay thee. Said (the other), Allah only accepts from those who are righteous. If thou dost stretch forth thy hand against me to slay me, I am not one-to stretch forth my hand against thee to slay thee, for I do fear Allah, the Lord of the worlds. Surely I wish that thou shouldst bear the sin committed against me as well as thy own sin and become of the inmates of the fire and this is the recompense of the unjust. Then his mind led him to the murder of his brother and so he murdered him and became one of the losers. Then Allah sent a raven who scratched the earth to show him how to conceal any flaws of his brother. He said: Woe is me! Was I not even able to be like this raven to conceal the flaws of my brother? So he became of those who regret. For this reason did We ordain for the children of Israel that whoever slays a soul unless it be for murder or for spreading mischief in the land, it would be as though he slew all men; and whoever keeps it alive, it would be as though he kept alive all men; and certainly Our apostle came to them with clear arguments but even after that many of them continued to commit excesses in the land. (v. 27-32).

In these verses the names of the two sons of Adam are not mentioned. The Qur'an calls all men as the sons of Adam as in "O Sons of Adam! When apostles come to you from amongst you." (vii. 35)

Therefore, it is not correct to say that the two sons mentioned in these verses were really the immediate descendants of Adam. The names of Habil and Qabil given in the commentaries are based on Jewish traditions Hassan and Zuhaq, two of the earliest commentators of the Qur'an have written that these two so-called sons of Adam were two Israelites only and the context of these verses supports this statement as the preceding and the following verses speak of the Israelites only.

This story is told in the Bible in Genesis, 4: 3-15, where Habil is called Abel and Qabil Cain. But a comparison of both the narratives will disclose that the Bible story differs in many respects with the one given in the Qur'an. There it is a bare narrative whereas the story as told by the Qur'an is pregnant with lessons.

This story is mentioned in the Qur'an to be taken allegorically to refer to the Jewish plot against the Holy Prophet where the Israelites may be taken as the aggressive and sinful brother and the Ishmaelites as represented by the Holy Prophet for the righteous one.

Abel's speech is full of meaning. He is innocent and God-fearing. To the threat of death held out by the other, he returns a calm reply aimed at reforming the other. But this had no effect on the elder brother who was full of pride, selfishness and jealousy. But after the murder was committed, the thought of slaying an innocent and righteous brother annoyed the murderer, specially when he observed how the raven hinted to him how to conceal the imperfections of his brother. The incident of the raven is not mentioned in the Bible story and the version of the Qur'an does not show that the raven scratched the earth to bury his companion who was dead, neither do ravens do such things. The concluding words of the story refer to the plight of the Israelites who rebelled against God, slew and insulted righteous men who did them no harm but on the contrary came to show them the way of rectitude in all humility. When God withdrew the favours from Israel because of their sins and bestowed them on a brother nation, the jealousy of Israel plunged them deeper into sin. To kill or to seek to kill an individual because he represents an ideal is to kill all who uphold that ideal. On the other hand, to save an individual life in the same circumstances is to save a whole community.

III. The Story of the Sabbath Breakers

(3) And well you know those among you who exceeded the limits of the Sabbath. So We said to them: Be (as) apes, despised and hated. So We made it an example to the people of their own time and those who came after it and an admonition to those who fear (the punishment) of God. (ii 65-66)

(4) And ask them about the town which stood by the sea. They exceeded the limits of the Sabbath when the fish came to them on the day of their Sabbath openly holding up their heads, but on the day they had no Sabbath they did not turn up thus did We try them because they were given to transgression. Therefore, when they insolently persisted

in what they had been forbidden. We said to them: Be as apes despised and hated. Thy Lord did declare that He would certainly send against them to the Day of Resurrection those who would subject them to severe torment. Most surely thy Lord is quick to requite (evil) and most surely He is Oft-Forgiving, Most Merciful. (vii. 163, 166-167)

The Jews and the Christians observed a particular day for religious worship and they were forbidden to do any work on that day. The punishment for breach of the Sabbath under the Mosaic Law was deth." Every one that defileth it (the Sabbath) shall surely be put to death: for whosoever doeth any work therein, that soul shall be cut off from among his people" (Exod. 31:14). This punishment was not for the breach of the Sabbath in itself but for the spirit of defiance of the Law. In this sense, there is no Sabbath among the Muslims, because in Islam no particular day is set apart for Divine worship. On the other hand, a Muslim is required to pray in the very midst of his everyday work and even the Friday prayer is no exception, for the Qur'an expressly allows the doing of work both before and after the Friday prayer. (See chapter lxii. 9-10).

The story to which this passage refers is as follows: In the days of David some Israelites dwelt at Ailah or Elath on the Red Sea, where on the night of the Sabbath the fish used to come in great number to the shore and stay there all the Sabbath to tempt them. But ,the night following, they returned to the sea again. A time came when some of the inhabitants neglecting God's command caught fish on the Sabbath and dressed and ate them, and afterwards becoming more greedy cut canals from the see and fitted sluices in them, so that after the fish entered the canals the sluices could be let down and the fish stopped from going back to sea at the end of the Sabbath. The other part of the inhabitants who strictly observed the Sabbath used both persuasion and force to stop this impiety but to no purpose, the offenders only growing more and mere obstinate where-upon David cursed the Sabbath breakers.

The Sabbath breakers were not metamorphosed into apes but they were morally reduced to the level of apes. A comparison of this verse may be made with verse v. 60 wherein it is said "(Worse

is he) whom Allah has cursed and brought His wrath upon him
and of whom He made apes and swine and who serveth the devil;
such are in worse plight and more erring from the straight path."
This description of the same people clearly shows that the
metamorphosis of men is not meant. Similarly, it is said in iv. 47:
"Or We shall curse them as We cursed that violators of the
Sabbath." Now, in the case of the Holy Prophet's opponents from
among the Jews who are referred to the words: "We shall curse
them," there is no mention of metamorphosis but here it is stated
that the same curse must overtake them as overtook the violators
of the sabbath. A reference to Deutronomy, Chap. 28, will show
that the curse which Moses prophesied for them meant their being
scattered among the nations of the earth, and this was the fate
which overtook the Prophet's enemies from among the Jews.

Turning to the Bible we find that the Israelites became apes
in all the senses in which that word is used in the Arabic language
by violating the Divine Commandments.

> Thou hast despised mine holy things, and hast profaned
> my sabbaths. In thee are men that carry tales to shed blood:
> and in thee they eat upon the mountains: in the midst of
> thee they commit lewdness. In thee have they discovered
> their fathers' nakedness: in thee have they humbled her
> that was set apart for pollution. And one hath committed
> abomination with his neighbour's wife; and another hath
> lewdly defiled his daughter in law; and another in thee
> hath humbled his sister, his father's daughter...and I will
> scatter thee among the heathen, and disperse thee in the
> countries. (Ezek. 22: 8-15)

IV. The Story of the Companions of the Cave

The account given about the Companions of the Cave in the
Qur'an is as follows:

> (5) Dost thou think that the companions of the cave and the
> inscription were of our wonderful signs? When the youths
> sought refuge in the cave they said: Our Lord! Grant us
> mercy from Thee and provide for us a right course in our
> affairs.
>
> Then We prevented them from hearing in the cave for a
> number of years. Then We raised them up that We might

know which of the two parties was best able to compute
the time for which they tarried there.

We relate to thee their story with truth. Surely they were
youths who believed in their Lord and We increased them
in guidance, and We strengthened their hearts with
patience when they stood up and said: Our Lord is the
Lord of the heavens and the earth. Never shall we call
upon any god other than He, for then indeed we should
have uttered an enormity. These our people have taken
gods besides Him. Why do they not bring forward any
clear authority in their support. Who is then more unjust
than he who forges a lie against Allah?

(Then they counselled among themselves:) When you
forsake them and what they worship besides Allah, betake
yourselves to the cave. Your Lord will shower His mercies
on you and provide for you a profitable course in your
affairs.

And thou wouldst have seen the sun when it rose declining
to the right of the cave and when it set turning away from
them to the left while they lay in the open space thereof.
Such are among the signs of Allah; whosoever Allah
guides, he is the rightly-guided and whomsoever Allah
leaves to stray, thou shalt not find any friend to lead him
to the right way.

And thou mightest think them awake, whilst they were
asleep and We turned them on their right and on their
left while their dog lay out stretching its paws at the
threshold.

If thou hadst come on them, thou wouldst certainly have
turned back from them in flight and wouldst certainly have
been filled with awe on their account. Thus did We raise
them that they might question each other. A speaker
amongst them said: "How long have you stayed here?"
They said: (Perhaps) a day or part of a day. They said:
Allah knows best how long you stayed here. Now send
one of you with this silver to the town and left him find
out which is the best food and bring some of it to you
and let him behave with gentleness and let not your case
make known to anyone, for if they should prevail against

you they would stone you to death or force you to return
to their creed. In that case you would never attain
prosperity.

Thus We made their case known to the people that they
might know that the promise of Allah is true and that there
can be no doubt the hour of judgement.

(When they were known) people began to dispute among
themselves about their affair. (Some) said: Construct a
building over them; their Lord knows best about them.
Those who prevailed over their affair said: "Let us surely
build a place of worship over them."

Some say they were three, their dog being the fourth,
others say they were five, their dog being the sixth,
doubtfully guessing at the unknown. (Yet others) say they
were seven, their dog being the eighth. Say thou: My Lord
knoweth best their number. It is but few who knew their
real case. Do not enter into controversies concerning them
except on a matter that is clear nor question any of them
about their affair.

And do not say of anything: Surely I shall do it tomorrow
without adding if Allah please, and call thy Lord to mind
when thou forgettest and say I hope that my Lord will
guide me closer even that this to the right course.

So they stayed in their cave three hundred years and
(some) add nine more. Say Allah knows best how long
they stayed. With Him is the knowledge of the secrets of
the heavens and the earth; how clear His sight and how
clear His hearing, nor does He share His command with
any other whatsoever, (xviii. 9-26)

The disbelievers among the Quraish were in the habit of putting
posers to the Holy Prophet, questions which they got from
Christians and Jews which they thought the Prophet would be
unable to answer. In this way they hoped to discredit him, One
of these questions was about the floating Christian legend of the
seven sleepers of Ephesus. The Prophet not only told them the
main story but pointed out the variations that were current and
rebuked men for disputing about details concerning them. He
treated the story as a parable providing spiritual lessons of the
highest value, giving hints about the coming events in the life of
the Prophet himself.

The bare Christian story is told in Gibbon's *Decline and Fall of the Roman Empire* (end of chapter 33). In the reign of a Roman Emperor who persecuted the Christians seven Christian youths of Ephesus left the town and hid themselves in a cave in a mountain nearby. They fell asleep and remained asleep for some generations or centuries. When the wall which sealed up the cave was demolished the youths awoke. They still thought of the world in which they had previously lived. They had no idea of the passage of time. But when one of them went to the town to purchase provisions he found that the whole world had changed. The Christian religion instead of being persecuted was fashionable and in fact it had become the state religion. His dress and speech and the money which he brought seemed to belong to another world. This attracted attention. The great ones of the land visited the cave and verified the tale by questioning the man's companions.

When the story became very popular and circulated throughout the Roman Empire, we may well suppose that an inscription was put up at the mouth of the cave.

A popular story circulating from mouth to mouth would necessarily be vague as to dates and its versions would vary very much in details. Somewhere about the sixth century C.E. a Syriac writer reduced it to writing. He suggested that the youths were seven in number, that they went to sleep in the reign of the Emperor Decius who reigned from 249 to 251 C.E. and who was a violent persecutor of Christianity, and that they awoke in the reign of the Emperor Theodosius II who reigned from 408 to 450 C.E. According to this the sleepers remained in the cave only for about 200 years, whereas the Qur'an mentions 300 years as the duration of their sleep. This mistake in the Christian traditions crept in on account of the name of the Roman Emperor called Decius. But from the letters of Pliny the younger, which he wrote to the Emperor Tarjan who ruled from 99 to 100 which have recently been discovered, a flood of light is thrown on the condition and treatment of the Christians in his time. In the reign of this monarch the seven youths of Ephesus went underground.

Tarjan after his conquest of Decia (modern Rumania) took the tile of Deciacus and got it inscribed on his coins. Hence the mistake of identifying Decius with Deciacus crept in. From the reign of this Deciacus to the reign of Tehodosis II three hundred years can be plainly counted. Is this not a miracle of the Qur'an that it has corrected the mistake of a popular tradition which none knew, until recent researches in Roman history were made? Further the Qur'an has related that a Church was built over the cave with an inscription thereon. This does not exist now but it did exist when the crusaders encamped at this place in the twelfth century. They found a church there called the Church of Seven Sleepers, built by Justinian. They are not the only people who had noted it. More than one Arab geographers and travellers have noted it too. How did the Prophet know of all this except through Divine revelation is a point for the Christians to ponder upon.

This story allegorically is taken to depict the state of Christianity in its early stages when the religion of Christ was propagated for about three hundred years in secrecy for fear of persecution by the Roman Emperors. It was after the conversion of Constantine in 325 C.E. that Christianity was openly preached, but then it had assumed the form of Trinity. Life in the cave for three hundred years may refer to the time when Christianity was not openly professed or preached. The special mention of the addition of nine years to three hundred seems to be due to their reduction to lunar years. It is recognised by Christian Divines that the Christian Era which is supposed to begin from the birth of Jesus did not actually do so, Jesus being born some six years prior to its commencement. Therefore 325 C.E. the date of the promulgation of the Nicene creed and the conversion of Constantine would then be actually 331 C.E. According to the Bible Jesus claimed his prophethood when he was thirty years old. In this way Christianity remained as the religion of the Unity of God for about three hundred years only. The Qur'an, by mentioning nine more years, separately, has indicated that according to lunar years the cave life of Christianity covered a period of three hundred and nine lunar years.

In this story there are prophetic allusions to the events of the Holy Prophet's life. In the words: "I hope that my Lord will guide me closer even than this to the right course" (xviii. 24) is a reference to the Prophet's taking refuge in a cave.

The difficulties which had to be experienced by the early Christians would be removed from the Prophet's way. He had to pass only three days in the cave and though a powerful enemy exerted itself to its utmost, his hiding place at only a distance of three miles from the city could not be discovered. Whereas it took three hundred years for Christianity to come out of the cave, Islam in three hundred years became a great religion of the world.

V. The Story of Khwajah Khidr and Moses

In the story of Moses we have purposely omitted to include this episode with the object of discussing it in fuller detail in connection with the story of Khwajah Khidr.

Moses wanted to explore some mysteries of life. He searched out a man endowed with knowledge derived from the Divine springs from which flow the paradoxes of life. He is shown three such paradoxes and how human impatience is inconsistent with their true understanding. The highest knowledge comes only as a Divine gift and by constant and patient striving with faith to apprehend something of the purpose of the All-Wise God. This is described in the following verses of the Qur'an. The story of this journey of Moses is not found in the Bible or even in the Rabbinicall literature but the latter relates things about Moses which give us a strong reason to believe that such a journey was undertaken by him. Here is what the Qur'an says:

(6) And Musa said to his servant: I will not give up this journey until I reach the junction of the two rivers though I march on for ages.

And when they reached the junction they forgot about their fish which being free took its way into the waters. But when they had gone farther he said to his servant: Bring to us our breakfast, for we have suffered much fatigue from this our journey. He replied: Didst thou see, when we took refuge on the rock I forgot about the fish--none but the devil made me forget to tell thee about it, and it took its way into the waters. What a wonder! He said: That was what we sought for. So they went back on their footsteps (following the path they had come).

Then they found one of Our servants on whom We had bestowed mercy from Us and whom We had given knowledge from Our presence.

Musa said to him: May I follow thee on condition that thou teach me something of the higher truth which thou has been taught? He said: Verily thou wilt not be able to bear

with me. And how canst thou have patience about things
about which thy understanding is not comprehensive? He
said: If Allah please, thou wilt find me patient and I shall
not disobey thee in aught. He said: If thou would follow
me ask me no questions about anything until I myself
speak to thee about it.

So they both proceeded until they were in the boat when
he scuttled it. Musa said: Hast thou scuttled it in order
to drown its inmates? Truly a strange thing has thou done.
He answered: Did I not tell thee that thou canst have no
patience with me? Musa said: Rebuke me not for forgetting
nor grieve me by raising difficulties in my case.

Then they proceeded until when they met a young man;.
he slew him. Musa said: Hast thou slain an innocent
person who had slain none? Truly thou has done an evil
thing. He answered: Did I not tell thee that thou canst
have no patience with me? Musa said: If ever I ask thee
about anything after this, keep me not in thy company.
Indeed thou shalt have then found an excuse in my case.
Then again they proceeded, until when they came to the
people of a town; they ask them for food but they refused
them hospitality. They found there a wall on the point of
falling down but he repaired it. Musa said: If thou hadst
wished, surely thou coulds have exacted some recompense
for it. He answered: This is the parting between me and
thee. Now will I tell thee the significance of those things
over which thou wast unable to hold thy patience. As for
the boat, it belonged to some poor men who worked on
the river. I only wished to render it unserviceable, for there
was after them a king who seized every boat by force. As
for the youth, his parents were people of faith and we
feared that he would bring upon them rebellion and
ingratitude. So we desired that their Lord would give them
in exchange a son better in purity and closer in affection.
As for the wall, it belonged to two orphan boys in the
city and there was beneath it a treasure to which they were
entitled and their father was a righteous man. So thy Lord
desired that they should attain their maturity and take out
their treasure--a mercy from thy Lord. And I did not do

it of my own accord. Such is the significance of those things over which thou wast unable to hold patience. (xviii. 60-82)

The story ends here. There is no mention of the name of the servant of God who was endued with mercy and knowledge from God. But in the traditions of the Prophet he is called Khidr which means green signifying that his knowledge is fresh and green and drawn out of the living sources of life, for it is drawn from God's own resence. He is a mysterious being who is to be sought out. He holds the secret of the paradoxes of life which ordinary people do not understand. Moses was to go and find a servant of God who would instruct him in such knowledge as he had not already got. He was to take a fish with him. The place where he was to meet his mysterious teacher would be indicated by the fact that the fish would disappear on his arrival at that place. The fish is the emblem of the fruit of secular knowledge which merges itself in Divine knowledge at the point were human intelligence is ready for the junction of the two. But the mere merger of secular knowledge does not itself produce Divine knowledge. The latter has to be sought patiently.

The phrase *Majma'-ul-Bahrain* does not indicate merely a junction of two rivers but it signifies the fact the two rivers must lose their identity as if they had fallen into the sea. There are many conjectures regarding the location of this place, but the most probable one seems to be the place where the river Jhelum and Sindh (not Indus) meet and after a few miles they fall into Wuller lake. At this junction and in mid-stream is a rock on which a platform has been made. It is locally known as "Muqam-i-Musa," the resting place of Moses and sometimes it is called "Kunah-i-Musa," the cornerstone of Moses. Thus it seems that Moses with his companion came to this junction and they took refuge on the rock and it was from this place that they retraced their steps. On their return journey Moses, meets Khwajah Khidr and asks permission to follow him. On their journey Khidr damages a boat and explains later that he did it to avoid its forcible seizure by a king.

Nalsain, king of Kashmir, according to the calculations of Wilson, was a contemporary of Moses. He was wicked and cruel. During his reign Kashmir was invaded and there was also a rebellion in the land Nalsain took forcible possession of all the good boats so that he might cut the means of communication of his enemies. This is a fact of history and Khwajah Khidr was made aware of the evil intentions of Nalsain (*Vide* H.H. Wilson, *Ancient History of Kashmir*, p. 81).

Josephus also records that Moses took leave of his people and went to Mount Nebu (*vide Josephus Antiquities*, iv, 8, 48). This mount Nebu is in Kashmir near Bandipur. It is reported in Bukhari, Vol. 2, 16, by Abu Hurairah that "When Moses's death approached he prayed to God to be permitted to see 'the Promised Land'. This prayer was granted. He (Moses) died there, 'If I were there,' the Prophet declared, 'I could have pointed out to you his tomb on the path of a rugged hill.'"

There is a further evidence to be noted in the very name of Khwajah Khidr. This is a very popular name among Kashmiris and Khwajah remaining "master" is prefixed to the names of respectable Kashmiris.

This episode in the story of Moses is meant to illustrate three points: (1) Moses was learned in all the wisdom of the Egyptians, but his wisdom did not comprehend everything. Divine knowledge as far as man is concerned is unlimited and constant effort is necessary to keep our knowledge square with the march of time and such an effort Moses is shown to be making (2) The mysterious man he meets to whom Tradition assigns the name of Khidr represents the type of that knowledge which is ever-green, fresh and flourishing. He had two special gifts from God, Mercy from His own presence, and Knowledge form His own presence. Moses, not understanding the full import of what he was asking for, makes a simple request. He wants to learn something of the spiritual knowledge which God had bestowed on Khidr. Khidr smiles and says that there will be many things which Moses will see with him which he will not completely understand and will make him impatient. The highest spiritual knowledge often seems paradoxical to those who have not the key to it. (3) The three paradoxes in life which eventually presented themselves in the course of their journey were: (a) Apparent loss may be real gain. The beneficent hand of God that works in nature is always directing humanity to the goal of great good though that good must necessarily be reached with apparent loss. This apparent loss in the case of the boat served a good purpose and brought much benefit to the owners. (b) Apparent cruelty may be real mercy. Life has to be sacrificed for the ultimate good of humanity at large. (c) The third instance shows that for the good of humanity deeds must be done which bring no immediate reward, and that good done by one generation is not devoid of benefit to the next. Sometimes returning good for evil may really be justice and not generosity. God's wisdom transcends all human calculations.

Moses himself had, in fact, to undergo the experience of his teacher and the incidents seem no more than prophetic allegories of Moses's own life-work. Just like the scuttling of the boat which caused apprehension to the safety of its inmates, Moses had to lead his people to a place where they thought they had only been brought to be drowned. But their safe passage through the water showed that it was for their good. Then he had to order his men to fight against iniquitous people and to put them to death, but he was not shedding human blood to no purpose, for it was reality a step towards the evolution of a better race. And finally his laying down his own life for the Israelites corresponded to his teacher's building the wall for the orphans without claiming recompense.

Again these incidents allegorically fit in with the prophetic mission of the Prophet Muhammad himself, and this appears to be the greatest reason why they are so categorically mentioned in the Qur'an. The first incident preventing the boat to be seized by force by making it unserviceable refers to the desert land of Arabia from where the glorious sun of Islam rose to dispel the darkness of ignorance and iniquity which enveloped the world. Being a desrt land, Arabia provided no attraction to the conquerors of the world and hence here people remaining free from foreign domination and conflicting philosophies and sophistry were the fittest to bear the universal message of God. All other nations of the world who were living under some kind of bondage in a state of self-imposed ignorance and inanity except for the ideas their masters wanted to infuse into them to make them serve their selfish interests and therefore they were incapable of bearing or spreading the universal message of Islam, which meant divinely-regulated liberty, fraternity, equality and the highest philosophy of life to enabling it to rise to the highest level of temporal and spiritual power.

In the second instance of slaying the youth, apparently

innocent, but actually a curse to humanity, is a response to those critics of the Prophet who blame him for slaying the Jewish leader of Medina who had become the inveterate enemies of the Prophet conspiring by all means at their disposal to crush the Muslim community at Medina and prevent the spread of Islam. Their extirpation from Medina was the most expedient measure of the day to get rid of their machinations against truth and justice.

The third instance of doing service without compensation for the future good of the orphans has a parallel in the person of the Prophet who exerted almost all his life to lift up his people from the degradation into which they had fallen in spite of their cruel treatment to him, and who lived the life of an ascetic in spite of the more than kingly power he weilded over the whole of Arabia, and whose heart always sank at the distress of humanity, and whose mercy never made any distinction between friend and foe. In the two orphans whose treasure was lying hidden under the wall is an allusion to the Jews and the Christians whose righteous ancestor was Moses and in setting the wall straight is an allusion to the recognition of the Torah and the Evangel as Divinely-inspired scriptures and in the treasure underlying the wall is an allusion to the suppressed prophecies in these books about the advent of the last Prophet which will one day surely be owned by these nations as proving the truth of the Prophet's calm.

VI. The Story of Dhulqarnain

(7) And they ask thee about Dhulqarnain Say: I shall recite to you some account of him Surely. We established him in the land and granted him means of access to everything. One such way he followed, until when he reached the place where the sun (appeared to) set, he found it going down into muddy black waters and near it he found a people. We said: O Dhulqarnain! (Thou has authority) either to punish them or to treat them with kindness. He said: Whoever doeth wrong, shall we punish him, and then he shall be sent back to his Lord and He will punish him with an exemplary punishment.

But whoever believeth and doeth that which is good, he shall have a generous recompense, and We will lay on him Our easy behests.

Then he followed (another) course, until he reached the land of the rising sun; he found it rising on a people for whom We provided no shelter from it. He left them as they were. He completely understood what was before him.

Then he followed another course until when he reached (a place) between the two mountains; he found beneath them a people who scarcely understood a word. They said: O Dhulqarnain! The Gog and Magog do great mischief in the land. Shall we then pay three tribute in order that thou mightest erect a barrier between us and them? He said: That in which my Lord hath established me is better (than your tribute). Help me therefore with labour and I will erect a strong barrier between you and them. Bring me blocks of iron.

At length when he had filled up the space between the two steep mountain sides, he said: Blow (with your bellows). Then when he had made it (red) as fire, he said: Bring me molten brass that I may pour over it. Thus they were made powerless to scale it or to dig through it. He said: This is a mercy from my Lord, but when the promise of my Lord come to pass, He will make it level with the ground and the promise of my Lord is ever true. (xviii-83-98)

These three episodes in the life of a great king Dhulqarnain illustrate how power and opportunities should be used in the service of God. He punished the guilty and rewarded the righteous. He left primitive people their freedom of life and he protected industrious people from their mischievous neighbours. With all the power and means at his command, he never became proud but submissively relied upon God and made his people remember the Day of Judgement when all will see the Truth and receive the punishment or reward earned in their present life.

The word "Dhulqarnain" is not a name but a title which means "the two-horned one" or "the Lord of the two epochs". Who was he? In what age and where did he live? The Qur'an gives us no material on which we can base a positive answer to these questions. Nor is it necessary to find an answer as the story is told for the lessons it provides. But popular opinion of the commentators identifies Dhulqarnain with Alexander the Great. But Alexander is an historical figure who, we know, believed in the Graecian gods. He considered himself a son of Jupiter Ammon (who had the two horns of a ram) But the Dhulqarnain of the Qur'an is a believer in God a just and righteous monarch, not selfish and greedy of conquest but a protector of the weak.

The three expeditions which are discribed in the Qur'an embody a great ethical idea involved in the possession of kingship or power. Therefore it is not correct to identify him with Alexander, the Macedonian king.

There is another suggestion put up by commentators that it was not the Macedonian Alexander but an earlier prehistoric king, a contemporary of Abraham.

From the note in *The Jewish Encyclopaedia and The Encyclopaedia Britannica* it may be safely concluded that Dhulqarnain was none other than Cyrus who ruled over a vast empire in the fifth century B.C. bounded on the west side by the Black Sea, and on the east by the deserts of Sind and Baluchistan, and on the north by the Caucasus mountains. He was a true follower of the Persian prophet Zoroaster and a contemporary of the Prophet Ezekiel. The tribes that lived beyond the Caucasus are called Gog and Magog in the Bible (Ezekiel. 38:39) as also in *The Jewish Encyclopaedia*. Josephs identifies them with the Scythians.

The three journeys alluded to seem to have been undertaken with the object of strengthening the frontiers of the empire, the most important of these being directed to that part of the frontier between the Caspian and the Black Sea where the Caucasus afforded a natural protection against the attacks of the Scythians, Cyrus goes first westward to the Black Sea, then eastward, and lastly northward to Mount Caucasus.

The barrier got up by Dhulqarnain is the famous wall at Derbend. We find in *The Encyclopaedia Britannica* the following passage about this wall: "And to the south lies the seaward extremity of the Caucasian wall (50 miles long otherwise known is 'Alexander's wall' blocking up the narrow pass of the Iron Gate or Caspian Gate. This wall had a height of 29 feet and a thickness of about 10 feet and with its iron gates and numerous watch-towers formed a valuable defence of the Persian frontier."

The misnomer "Alexander's wall" seems to have been due to the mistake made by Muslim historians in supposing Dhulqarnain to be Alexander.

As regards Gog and Magog a further reference has come in the chapter entitled "the Prophet," verse 96, which states: "Even when Gog and Magog are let loose and they shall break froth from every elevated place." It is said in one of the traditions of the Prophet that no nation of the world shall be able to fight with the Gog and Magog who will occupy all positions of vantage on the earth, and become its rulers. Then they will fight among themselves and destroy each other. The Slaves of Russia and the Teutonic races that occupy Europe and America may be indentified with the Gog and Magog of the Qur'an and the traditions of the Prophet.

VII. The Story of Qarun (Korah)

Qarun or Korah is mentioned in the Qur'an in three places. In chapter entitled "Believer" (23-24) it is said:

(8) And certainly We sent Musa with Our communications and clear authority to Fir'aun and Haman and Qarun but they said: A lying enchanter.

This shows that among those who belied Moses Korah was also an important figure. In the chapter entitled "Spider" (39-40). It is said:

(9) And We destroyed Qarun and Fir'aun and Haman and certainly Musa came to them with clear argument but they behaved haughtily in the land; yet they could not outstrip Us. So each We punished for his sin and of them was he on whom We sent down a violent storm and of them was he whom the rumbling overtook, and of them was he whom We made to be swallowed up by the earth and of them was he whom We drowned and it did not beseem Allah that He should be unjust to them but they were unjust to their own souls.

In this passage also Korah is mentioned along with Pharaoh and Haman and the words "of them was he whom We made to be swallowed up by the earth" refer to the death of Korah. But in the chapter entitled 'The Narrative' (76-82) some more details are given about Korah.

(10) Surely Qarun was of the people of Musa, but he rebelled against them and We had given him of the treasures so much so that his hoards of wealth would certainly weigh down a company of man possessed of great strength.

When his people said to him: Do not exult, surely Allah does not love the exultant. And seek by means of what Allah has given thee the future abode and do not neglect thy portion of this world and do good (to others) as Allah has done good to thee and do not seek to make mischief in the land. Surely Allah does not love the mischief-makers.

He said: I have been given this only on account of the knowledge I have. Did he not know that Allah had destroyed before him of the generations, those who were mightier in assemblage? And the guilty shall not be asked about their faults.

So he went forth to his people in his finery. Those who desire this world's life said: O! would that we had the like of what Qarun is given. Most surely he is possessed of mighty good fortune. But those who were given true knowledge said: Woe to you! Allah's reward is better for him who believes and does good and none is made to receive this except the patient.

Thus We made the earth to swallow up him and his abode; so he had nobody of helpers to assist him against Allah, nor was he of those who can defend themselves. And those who yearned for his place only the day before began to say: Ah! (Know) that Allah amplifies and straitens the means of subsistence for whom He pleases of His servants. Had not Allah been gracious to us, He would most surely have abased us. Ah! (Know) that the ungrateful are never successful.

The story of Korah, his revolt against the leadership of Moses and Aaron and his being swallowed up by the earth is given in the Old Testament, Numbers, Chapter 16, without giving any reference to his wealth. But the Qur'an mentions his wealth to be so enormous that it took many strong men to carry the keys of his treasure chests. The fact of his great wealth mentioned in the Qur'an is corroborated by the exaggerated description of the Jewish Midrashim which shows that the weight of the keys of his treasure chests was equivalent to the load of 300 mules. Here is one more instance of the Divine sources of the Qur'anic revelation which clearly refutes the allegations of the Christian critics that the Qur'an borrows its stories from the Bible.

There are several moral lessons that can be derived from the above story. If wealth is not used properly there are three evils that follow: (1) Its possessor becomes miser and forgets the claims of his self and also of those about him. (2) He forgets the poor and the needy and the good cause which deserve and require monetary support. (3) He misspends no occasions causing a great deal of harm and mischief. Apparently Korah had all the three vices. He had become so blind and arrogant that he thought that his own merit, knowledge and skill or cleverness had earned him his wealth and that on account of it he was superior to everybody else and was entitled to ride roughshod over them. When he was in the heyday of his glory worldly people envied him and thought how happy they would be if they were endowed like him. But those who had true knowledge knew of a more precious and lasting wealth--the reward of God in the Hereafter which is reserved for the righteous. Material wealth after all is fleeting and a temptation and a cause of fall.

When his fall came, the rabble that admired Korah's wealth when he was in worldly prosperity sees the other side of the question and understands that there are other gifts more precious and lasting and that these may actually be withheld from men who enjoy wealth and worldly prosperity. In fact it is false prosperity in the real sense of the word which is without spiritual well-being. It is the righteous who win in the end.

VIII. The Story of Luqman

'Any historical fact related by oriental people is a myth in the terminology of the "broadminded" Europeans while the most absurd myths of Europe are considered very reliable history. The sage Luqman belongs to Arab tradition and a chapter of the Qur'an is named after him. Very little is known of his life. Many instructive apologues are credited to him, similar to Æsop's fables in Greek tradition and, therefore, some people identify Luqman with Æsop, but there is no historical evidence to justify such an identification.

(11) And certainly We bestowed wisdom on Luqman saying: Be grateful to Allah and whoever is grateful does to the profit of his own self, and whoever is ungrateful, surely Allah is Self-Sufficient, Worthy of all Praise.

Behold, Luqman said to his son by way of instruction: O

my son! Do not associate ought with Allah, for polytheism
is indeed the highest iniquity.

And We have enjoined on man to be good to his parents;
in travail upon travail does his mother bear him until his
weaning takes two years. Show gratitude to Me and to
thy parents and to Me is the eventual return. But if they
contend with thee that thou shouldst associate with Me
what thou hast no knowledge of, do not obey them, yet
keep company with them in this world with kindness and
consideration and follow the way of him who turns to Me.
In the end the return of you all is to Me and then I will
inform you of all that you did.

O my son! if there be the weight of a mustard seed even
though it were hidden in a rock or anywhere in the heaven
or on earth, Allah will bring it forth, for Allah understands
the finest subtleties and is well-acquainted with them. O
my son! establish regular prayers and enjoin what is best
and forbid what is wrong and bear with patient constancy
whatever betide thee, for this is firmness of purpose in
the conduct of affairs. And do not swell thy cheek (for
pride) at men nor walk in insolence in the land. Surely
Allah does not love any self-conceited boaster. And be
moderate in thy pace and lower thy voice, for the harshest
of sounds without doubt is the braying of asses. (xxxi. 12-
19)

Luqman is held up as a pattern of wisdom because he realised
the best in a wise life in this world as based upon the highest
hope in the inner life. To him, as in Islam, true human wisdom
is also divine wisdom: the two cannot be separated. The beginning
of all wisdom, therefore, is conformity with the Will of God which
means that we must understand our relations to Him and worship
Him aright. Then we must be good to mankind, beginning with
our own parents, for the two duties are not different but one. When
the duty to man conflicts with the duty to God, it means that there
is something wrong with the human will, and we should obey God
rather than man. Performance of duties does not mean that we
should be arrogant or insolent. To parents and those in authority,
we must be kind, considerate and courteous even when they
command things which we should not do though disobedience
becomes our highest duty.

The worship of things other than God is the Worship of false things which are alien to our true knowledge, things that go against our pure nature as created by God. In any apparent conflict of duties our standard should be God's will as declared to us by His command. That is the way of those who love God, and their motive in disobedience to parents or human authority where disobedience is necessary by God's Law, is not self-willed rebellion or defiance but love of God which means the true love of man in the highest sense of the word and the reason we should give is: "Both you and I have to return to God, therefore not only I must follow God's will but you must command nothing against God's will"

These conflicts may appear to us strange and puzzling this life. But in God's presence we shall see their real meaning and significance. It may be that was one way in which or true mettle could be tested, for it is not easy to disobey and love man at the same time.

The golden mean is the pivot of the philosophy of Luqman as it is of the philosophy of Islam, and it follows naturally from a true understanding of our relation to God and His universe and everything in it, specially man. In all things we should be moderate, neither running nor stationary, neither talkative nor silent, neither hoisterous nor timid and half-hearted, neither too confident nor diffident. If we have patience, it gives us constancy and determination so that we may bravely carry on the struggle of life. If we have humility, it saves us from unseemly swaggering and consequent envy and conflict and does not stand in the way of having the right spirit and reasoned determination.

The essence of the whole Sermon on the Mount is given here in a few words to show that God has not been partial in blessing only a single nation with high moral teachings. Even an Ethiopian could preach the meekness and humility of which the most materially advanced nations of the day may well feel proud.

IX. The Story of the Ashab-ul-Ukhdud (People of the Ditch)

The Qur'an turns another page of authentic history of the nations unknown to the Arabs in the following:

(12) By the heavens adorned with the signs of the Zodiac, by the promised day of Judgement; and by the witness and the witnessed, woe to the makers of the Pit (of fire) of

the fire supplied kept burning with fuel. Behold! They sat over against the fire and they witnessed all that they were doing against the believers and they did not take vengeance on them for aught except that they believed in Allah, the Mighty, the Praised, whose is the kingdom of the heavens and the earth and Allah is a witness of all things. Surely those who persecute the believing men and the believing women and afterwards repent not, for them is prepared the chastisement of hell and they shall suffer the pain of burning. (lxxxv. 1-10)

Who were these Ashab-ul-Ukhdud or people of the ditch or pit who burnt true believers? The Arabs did not know them, and they have made several guesses and drawn upon their own national folklore with regard to Dhu Nuwas of Yemen, forgetting that Dhu Nuwas, if existing at all, flourished long before Jesus, and that as a Jew he could not possibly be a ruler of any country as the Jews were deprived of this grace since their dispersion. Now we know that they were Roman Ceasars who persecuted Christians and Nero who actually used them as burning torches after the conflagration of Rome, for which they were falsely accused, and "Ukhdud" is the literal rendering of the Roman "Amphitheatre" which, as every student of Roman history knows, was built like a pit and the Christians were burnt alive in the arena of this Amphitheatre while all Rome sat rejoicing at the agony of burning humanity.

The question is who told the Prophet of the people of the Ditch; perhaps, as the Christians would say, some wretched Greek slaves that were brought to Mecca and sold there and bought by Muhammad for the sole purpose of learning Roman history!

X. The Story of the Ashab-ul-Fil (People of the Elephant)

(13) Seest thou not how thy Lord dealt with the companions of the elephant? Did he not cause their treacherous plan to end in confusion and send against them flights of birds striking them with stones of baked clay. So he rendered them like straw eaten up (cv. 1-5).

This Surah refers to an event that happened in the year of the birth of the Holy Prophet. Abrahah, the Christian viceroy of the king of Abyssinia at Yemen, wanted to destroy the Ka'bah in order to divert the Arab trade and religious enthusiasm to Saa'n' where he had built a magnificent cathedral. His army is known in Arabia as the Ashab-ul-Fil or the Companions of the Elephant because of the presence of elephants in the invading army. Unable to defend the holy place against the huge army and falling to dissuade Abrahah who was now encamped at a distance of some three days march from Mecca, from his sacrilegious purpose. 'Abdul Muttalib prayed aloud leaning upon the door of the Ka'bah: "Defend, O Lord! Thine Own House and suffer not the Cross to triumph over the Ka'bah". And then the whole population of Mecca repaired to the hills around the holy city. Meanwhile a shower of stones dropped by flocks of birds destroyed the invading army almost to a man. The stones produced a disease of sores and pustules on the skin which spread like pestilence. There is another version of this story by the historians Waqidi and Ibn Hisham who attribute the cause of the destruction of Abrahah's army to smallpox. The mention of birds is merely intended to show that when they were dead the birds feasted on their corpses, tearing off flesh from the dead bodies and casting it on stones and that is why in the concluding words their dead bodies are compared to straw that is eaten up.

The lesson to be drawn from this story is twofold. For the Pagan Quraish of Mecca it was: God will protect his own; if you persecute the Holy Prophet he is greater than the mere edifice of Ka'bah: Will not God protect him?

For men in all ages the lesson is: a man intoxicated with power can prepare armies and material resources against God's holy plan, but his plan will work his own undoing; he cannot prevail against God.

XI. Conclusion

These are the stories given in the Qur'an with their sublime morals for the guidance of humanity, revealed to an Arabian living in a remote city isolated from the civilised world of fourteen centuries ago by vast stretches of sand deserts and about whom the Qur'an records:

> (14) And thou didst not read before it any book nor did thou write one with thy right hand, for, then, could those who say untrue things have doubted. (xxix. 48)

and yet the thick veils of prejudice and bigotry which have fallen
on the eyes of the unjust people do not let them see the truth
of his claim to Divine inspiration. Not only the truths of the
religious scriptures which were never read by the Holy Prophet
are to be found in the Holy Qur'an in their true colours devoid
of all extraneous absurd matter clogged round them by unchaste
hands but also other truths which are not to be found in any
scripture but are gradually coming to light after the strenuous
researches by the learned people of the world. What more
testimony is required to show that the source from which the Holy
Qur'an came was far above the knowledge possessed by human
being.

We shall conclude with a humble prayer taught by the Qur'an:

(15) Our Lord! Make not our hearts deviate after Thou hast
guided us aright and grant us from Thee Mercy. Surely
Thou art the most liberal Giver. (iii. 7)

INDEX